Cooking the One-Burner Way

Cooking the One-Burner Way

by
Melissa Gray *and* Buck Tilton

Globe Pequot Press
Old Saybrook, Connecticut

Cooking the One-Burner Way

10 9 8 7 6 5 4

Library of Congress Cataloging-in-Publication Data

Tilton, Buck.
    Cooking the one burner way: gourmet cuisine for the backcountry chef / by Buck Tilton and Melissa Gray.
        p. cm.
    Includes index.
    ISBN 0-934802-91-2 : $11.99
    1. Outdoor cookery. I. Gray, Melissa, 1960– . II. Title.
TX823.T55 1994
641.5'782—dc20
                                        93-50701
                                        CIP

Contents

To our moms, Elaine Dube and Eris Tilton, with great love and deep appreciation for the many years they fed us.

Acknowledgements

B ooks are seldom, if ever, the work of one or two people. An appeal to our friends for their favorite backcountry recipes, and other assistance, brought a foodbag of tasty responses. We especially thank: Kate Bartlett, Jerri Bell, Margaret Brady, Alexandra Conover, Kitty Ann and Roger Cox, Peter DeJung, Elaine Doll, Tamah Donaldson, Elaine Dube, Bethany Grohs and Justin Grohs, Barb Harper, Michael Hock, Ruthe Hubbell, Iretta Hunter, Lisa Jaeger, Brett LeCompte, Tim Lindholm, J. Scott McGee, Rob Meltzer, Steve Mital, Steve Platz and Shana Tarter, Daniel Robison, James Rosner, Jennifer Rouillard, Ben Sparks, Mark Stivers, Eris Tilton, David Tomco, Ronald Turner, Woodswomen, Inc., and, for tireless day-to-day effort, Lori "Spike" Patin.

Introduction

Not another outdoor cookbook! Well, yes . . . and no. Yes, even if you know how to cook outdoors, by the time you've digested all the information in this book you'll know how to cook outdoors better. So it's a cookbook. But, no, even if you know nothing about cooking outdoors, this book gives you all you need to know about choosing food and stoves and cookgear, about how much of what you'll need for so many days, about special considerations such as high altitude and extreme cold, about camp hygiene so you don't consume things that make you unhealthy, about leaving your campsite environmentally clean, and about preparing everything from yippee-ki-yay cowboy coffee to wild currant cottlestone pie via your choice of entrees. In short, this book gives you the opportunity to become a Backcountry Chef.

This book sits firmly on a one-burner backcountry-stove foundation. One-burner because such stoves are available, lightweight, compact and infinitely functional. Backcountry because Mother Earth has withstood too many open fires in too many places for too long a time. Although campfires are acceptable, or at least tolerated, in some places, with a one-burner you'll cook faster and be able to dine finely in areas with limited wood, such as above treeline. More and more Backcountry Chefs need to be taking only pictures and leaving only nothing.

Our longest one-burner trip was 62 days in Idaho's Frank Church-River Of No Return Wilderness, where a small Cessna dropped our re-supplies. The shortest was a one-nighter cooking off the tailgate of our Bronco, fishing the beaver ponds along Colorado's Middle Quartz Creek. In between lie over 40 combined years of boiling, baking, poaching and frying out of backpacks, canoe bags, seakayak bags and saddlebags. On many nights we've coaxed hot soup out of cold pots at 18,000 feet in Alaska and swatted mosquitoes while fresh fish sizzled in Florida. We've taught cooking to students from junior high schools, high schools, colleges, universities, Outward Bound, the National Outdoor Leadership School, the Wilderness Education Association, and the Boy Scouts.

Through hundreds and hundreds of backcountry days, we've progressed from solid lumps of scorched mac-and-cheese to fresh baked bread and delicately seasoned casseroles. This book will make your journey much shorter . . . and far more tasty. In the end we hope you'll have more fun eating better and taking better care of the backcountry.

Melissa Gray and Buck Tilton
Pitkin, Colorado - December 1993

Nutrition: Body Fuel

F ood, whatever its taste and psychological benefits, acts as fuel for the human engine, go-power, and the worth of the go is called its nutritional value. Nutrition, like politics, ends up being largely a matter of personal opinion, but a shortage of nutrients, despite who you voted for, causes everyone to have energy slumps that bring early fatigue, lassitude, mind-numbness and a predisposition for getting sick. Start every backcountry trip by planning to eat nutritionally well.

ENERGY SOURCES

Your body has three sources of energy: carbohydrates, fats and, to some extent, proteins. Although all food ends up being digested into simple compounds before it can be burned for power, *carbohydrates* (sugars and starches) digest the quickest and easiest. Simple carbohydrates (simple sugars: table sugar, brown sugar, date sugar, honey, molasses) are small molecular units that break down very fast, entering the bloodstream soon after you eat them. You get an energy boost right away. But most sugars are burned so quickly, energy levels can suddenly fall below your starting point if all you eat is simple carbohydrates. So complex carbohydrates (strings of simple sugars called starches) need to be a major portion of your diet. Being a more complex molecular unit, starches break down more slowly, providing power for the long haul. Carbohydrates should supply at least 60% of the calories in your backcountry diet.

COMPLEX CARBOHYDRATE SOURCES: whole grains and whole grain products (cereals, breads), pasta, fruits and vegetables.

Fat is necessary for a healthy life . . . but not much fat. In fact, your body will manufacture fat from carbohydrates and proteins if you run short. Your body worries about running out of fat so much that it'll store unbelievable quantities against a fatless day. Unfortunately and unhealthily, you don't know when you have too much of a good thing. Fat breaks down very slowly in the digestive process, so more time is required for it to provide energy. There are saturated fats and unsaturated fats, and most fats, animal and vegetable, are combinations of both kinds. Saturated fats are harder, and stick to your arteries better, and so they're considered less healthy than unsaturated fats. Cholesterol (lipoproteins) is a substance found in animal fats. Low density lipoproteins (LDL) seem to lend themselves to heart disease more than high density lipoproteins (HDL). HDLs have even been associated with a reduced risk of heart disease. Fats have a devilish quality: they tend to taste really good. But fats should supply only approximately 25% of your diet.

FAT SOURCES: butter, margarine, oils, cheeses, meats and nuts.

Proteins are made up of amino acids, and amino acids are the basic substance of human tissue. Proteins are not a primary energy source, but your body will use them if nothing else is available, or if you exercise for a long period of time. But, since tissue is continually lost and replaced (and new tissue is built when you exercise), proteins are essential to life. All of the amino acids are synthesized by your body, except for eight which have to be eaten. A "complete protein" has all eight of these amino acids. Eggs, milk and meat (including fish) are complete. Other foods, such as grains, seeds, nuts and legumes contain incomplete proteins, but since they're incomplete in different ways, some of them can be combined to form complete proteins. Legumes (soybeans, navy beans, kidney beans, pinto beans, lima beans, peanuts, black-eyed peas, chickpeas, split peas, lentils) combine with seeds and nuts to form complete proteins, and milk products and whole grains combine completely also. Most whole grains combine with most legumes to complete the protein package. Some milk products combine with some seeds and nuts to form complete proteins. Proteins need to make up about 15% of your diet.

PROTEIN SOURCES: meat, milk and milk products, eggs, seeds, nuts, legumes, whole grains.

Boost your protein intake by:

Combining rice with legumes, wheat, seeds or milk products (e.g. Instant Rice Pudding or Curried Rice).

Combining wheat with legumes, nuts, seeds or milk products (e.g. Pizza or Peanut Butter Bread).

Combining legumes with corn, seeds, whole grains or milk products (e.g. Falafel and Cheese Tortillas or Curried Lentils).

Combining seeds with milk products (e.g. Szechwan Noodles or Barb's Granola and Milk).

Combining potatoes and milk products (e.g. Bugg's Alpine Start or Spicy Shepherds Pie).

VITAMINS, MINERALS, FIBER

You won't function for long without **vitamins**, and these little organic molecules must be eaten. Vitamins are necessary for food to be processed into energy for life. There are 13 known vitamins. Some are fat-soluble (A, D, E, K), and are stored in fatty tissue and organ tissue of the body. Some are water-soluble (C and the Bs), cannot be stored, and wash out when you sweat or urinate. As long as you eat a balanced diet, you'll probably get the vitamins you need. On extended backcountry trips, you may consider taking a daily multi-vitamin that meets the recommended daily allowances (RDA) of the National Academy of Sciences. To exceed the RDA, especially with fat-soluble vitamins, may be harmful.

Traces of several **minerals** are also required for you to continue to function. These minerals are generally divided into two classes: 1) major minerals (such as calcium) that you need more of than 2) minor minerals (such as iron). Once again, a balanced diet supplies all the minerals you need. If you decide to take supplements, do not exceed the RDA. Remember: taking vitamin/mineral supplements is like trying to cheat your way to health. They are not a substitute for eating right.

Fiber is that stuff in some foods that you eat but don't digest, yet it plays a vital role in health. There are two kinds of fibers: insoluble (whole grain products, bran, cellulose) and soluble (oats, oat bran, fruits, vegetables, nuts, beans). Insoluble fiber won't hold much water, so it moves quickly through your digestive tract, and encourages other food to move quickly, keeping your bowel movements regular. Too much insoluble fiber may produce too much movement. Soluble fiber absorbs water and becomes gooey, sticking to other foods and slowing their assimilation into your body. This is healthy because soluble fibers stick to some potentially harmful cholesterol better than your body does, so it is carried out.

WATER

Water probably ranks as the most common thing your body needs more of. It is the most important nutrient that passes your lips, something you need almost as critically as air, the medium of energy production and body temperature control and waste removal of metabolic by-products. To feel well and perform well, you've got to drink a lot of water because you lose it constantly through sweat and urination and defecation, even through breathing.

Start each day with about a half quart, 16 ounces of water. During periods of exercise you should be downing about 8 more ounces every 15 or 20 minutes. For wilderness travel, and for life in general, the old piece of advice to drink enough water to keep your urine clear and copious rings with truth.

NUTRITION IN THE COLD OUTDOORS

Although your need for vitamins and minerals does not change, your need for water goes up and your energy requirements are increased in a cold environment. To meet the increased need, you should drink more and eat more. The single most important factor in cold-weather food consumption is carrying food you enjoy eating. The nutrient breakdown should be approximately the same: 60% carbohydrate, 25% fat, 15% protein. Carbohydrate intake is especially important to replenish muscle energy stores in order to prevent excess fatigue which often leads to cold injury. Cold tolerance may be improved for most people by a high-fat snack (about one-third the calories from fat) every couple of hours: one or two snacks between breakfast and lunch, another one between lunch and dinner, and one more before crawling into your sleeping bag. If you're one of those people who awake cold during the night, pack a snack into your sleeping bag. We like to make a water bottle of hot chocolate before bedtime. In the sleeping bag, it provides warmth by contact. Later in the night, it provides warmth by calories. (Make sure the top is screwed on tight!)

NUTRITION AT HIGH ALTITUDE

Higher altitudes tend to be cold, and the same cold-weather recommendations apply, with one exception: fat is not tolerated as well at higher altitudes—altitudes above 14,000 feet. Fat tolerances decrease as altitude increases. You will probably function better if you change high-fat snacks to high-energy, high-carbohydrate snacks. There is also some evidence indicating that people on high-carb diets—about 70% carbohydrate—acclimatize better to higher altitudes. Because altitude often affects your appetite, it is critical to carry food you crave. Proper nutrition is important, but not as important as an adequate caloric and fluid intake. And not as important as healthy physical conditioning, and proper clothing and gear.

Food and Menu Planning

GENERAL THOUGHTS

Whether it's a paddling weekend on the lakes of Minnesota or a month on a high Alaskan mountain, nothing upsets people faster than having too little or rotten-tasting food. Too much can be a problem too, especially if you're required to carry it or pull it, but it doesn't usually result in the death of the food packer/cook.

So here's some questions to ask yourself and your traveling companions before purchasing and packing the grub.

1. **How long will you be in the backcountry?** For short trips (less than a week) we tend to count the specific meals needed, pre-plan a menu, and repackage ingredients into a Bag-a-Feast per meal. On longer trips we package our food in bulk bags and plan our menus as we go. Both of these methods will be described in greater detail later in this chapter.

2. **What's the time of year and level of expected activity?** Cold weather and high intensity exercise will increase the caloric need of your body. Are you planning to fish or hunt? Fish can be a great supplement to a diet, but if you get skunked you can be very hungry. Trust us, it happens!

3. **Who's going with you?** A coed group of pre-adolescents eat far less than a group of guys in their twenties. Most small folks eat less than most large folks. People experienced with outdoor cooking and travel tend to eat more than novices (instructors vs. students). Some people just plain eat more than other people. When packing for groups, this usually evens out somewhere, otherwise "practice makes perfect."

4. **Does the group have any special needs?** Allergies, diabetes, religion and even likes and dislikes greatly affect what people will eat. An informal questionnaire is often helpful.

5. **How much money do you have?** Yes, you must have a certain amount, but by staying away from pre-packed meals and specialty items you sure save dollars as well as cutting down on wasteful packaging.

TOTAL RATION PLANNING VS. SPECIFIC MENU PLANNING

Basically you have two options for food and menu planning. We use them both regularly but in different situations.

OPTION 1: TOTAL RATION PLANNING

Total Ration Planning is our first choice for backcountry food planning. It works just as well for 2 folks on a ten-day Maine coastal kayaking trip as it does for a group of 12 backpackers crossing Utah's Grand Gulch.

Total Ration Planning grants you the freedom to pack a wide variety of dried foods allowing for endless meal options. When you menu plan as you go, instead of ahead of time, you are allowed to be spontaneous, adapting to the day's preferences and tasks. Food requirements change easily with the weather and your preferences.

Also, by cooking from scratch you minimize pre-packaged foods, increase nutrition, cut down on fat and salt, get to use your imagination, and, most important, impress your companions with your cooking prowess.

HOW DO I DO IT? IMPORTANT DETAILS

NUMBER OF DAYS(D): This is an easy one to figure but important to future calculations.

NUMBER OF PEOPLE WHO WANT TO EAT(P): Usually every one wants to eat. Don't trust them if they say they don't. Once they smell your cooking they'll change their mind.

CALORIC NEEDS AND WEIGHT(W): Some people work these out separately and specifically. We have had a lot of luck generalizing caloric intake and only starved to death once. (We got better later.) If you want to work out your caloric intake specifically, there is a chart in the appendix with the most commonly used backpacking foods and their corresponding calories per pound. There are several software programs available that make this task a breeze.

HOW MUCH FOOD DO YOU NEED?

Food equals weight. And the more energy you exert the more food you will need. Remember, extreme weather greatly increases your energy output. Below you will find four plans for different types of outdoor adventures. Read them and pick the one that closely resembles the trip you are currently planning.

PLAN 1: This plan is utilized in very warm conditions when you don't feel super hungry or when activity level is very low. For example: base camps or water trips where you supplement your diet with fishing and/or some fresh and canned food.

Pack 1.5 pounds of food per person per day. Calories will add up to roughly 2200-2500 per day.

PLAN 2: This is the plan we personally use most often. It keeps most folks content with the food supply on the average backcountry excursion from Spring through Fall.

Pack between 1.75 and 2.0 pounds of food per person per day. Calculated calories should add up to roughly 2500-3000 per day.

PLAN 3: This plan works best for folks who are traveling in cold environments or are putting in extremely heavy work days.

Pack 2.0-2.25 pounds of food per person per day. Calculated calories should add up to roughly 3000-3500 per day.

PLAN 4: This plan is utilized in only the most extreme environments: extreme cold, high altitude mountaineering, Continental Divide through-hikers, etc.

Pack 2.5 pounds of food per person per day or more. At this level eating becomes a discipline more than a result of hunger.

Example: 2 folks are taking a 10-day July backpacking and fishing trip in the Rockies. How much food do they need?

2 people(P) x 10 days(D) x 1.75 food/day(Plan 2) = 35.0 pounds of food

These folks need to pack 35 pounds of food total for their 10-day trip.

WHAT TO BRING: Types of Food

If you are inexperienced with backcountry cooking, we suggest bringing a wide variety of foods and a copy of this book. Then have fun.

We break our rationing down into 8 categories and distribute the food as follows:

1. BREAKFAST: About 15% of the total weight.
   Examples: Bagels, cream of wheat, Grapenuts, granola, hash browns, oatmeal.

2. DINNERS: About 20% of the total weight.
   Examples: Bulgur, couscous, dried potatoes, falafel, lentils, pasta, instant beans, rice, tortillas.

3. FLOUR: About 10% of total weight.
   Examples: Wheat, white, cornmeal, baking mix, muffin mix, bread mix.

4. HIGH FAT ITEMS: About 13% of total weight.
   Examples: Cheese, margarine, meats, oil, peanut butter.

5. MUNCHABLES: About 20% of total weight.
    Examples: Candy, crackers, dried fruit, fruit bars, high energy bars, pita bread, nuts and seeds, trail mix.

6. DRINKS AND SUGARS: About 10% of total weight.
    Examples: Sugar, fruit crystals, honey, hot chocolate, gelatin.

7. DESSERTS: About 3% of total weight.
    Examples: Brownie mix, cake mix, cheesecake mix, pudding mix.

8. MISCELLANEOUS: About 8% of total weight.
    Examples: Milk powder, soup mix, dried vegetables, egg powder, tomato base.

Total Ration Planning is not an exact science. If you add up the percentages in the eight categories, you will see that the grand total equals only 99%. This gives you a little freedom in packaging and planning. There is a lot of flexibility with the categories, but it is important your total weight measures up. If you come up light when you weigh your food bag, throw in a couple of your favorite items. If you come up heavy, get rid of something.

The more you use this method, the more you will learn the ins and outs of the foods that will most please you and your companions. If you are having trouble knowing where to begin, Table A will give you a general plan. The table is based on a ten-day ration for two folks so remember to adjust for number of days x number of people x number of lbs. per day to arrive at your grand total of food needed.

Non or low caloric items, although you need to bring them along, should not be counted in your total poundage. Examples of these items include: spices, bouillon cubes, hot sauce, coffee, items with Nutrasweet, small amounts of dried vegetables, etc.

Once you become more experienced with Total Ration Planning, feel free to substitute your favorite foods into the plan. But be careful to substitute foods of approximately equal caloric value. For example, if you substitute 2 pounds of cheese (3200 calories) with 2 pounds of tuna (1400), you will end up significantly reducing your total calories by 1800 calories. Additionally, many people decide not to bake. (We can't figure this one out!) Remember, if you're not going to bring flour you should consider substituting it with breads and crackers.

OPTION 2: SPECIFIC MENU PLANNING

Specific Menu Planning works well on short trips (less than a week) or when you have little time or energy to spend on food preparation in the field. Although it is not required, we almost always use this plan for high altitude or extremely cold weather

TABLE A: SAMPLE FOOD RATION PLAN

10/day ration for 2 people	1.5 lbs./ day/ person	1.75 lbs./ day/ person	2 lbs/day day/ person	2.25 lbs./ day/ person
TOTAL	**30 lbs.**	**35 lbs.**	**40 lbs.**	**45 lbs.**
BREAKFASTS				
% OF TOTAL LBS.	**15%**	**15%**	**15%**	**15%**
Bagels	1.0	1.0	2.0	2.0
Cream O Wheat		.5	.5	.5
Grapenuts	1.0	1.0	1.0	1.0
Granola	.5	.75	.5	1.25
Hashbrowns	1.0	1.0	1.0	1.0
Oatmeal	1.0	1.0	1.0	1.0
Subtotal	**4.5**	**5.25**	**6.0**	**6.75**
DINNERS				
% OF TOTAL LBS.	**20%**	**20%**	**20%**	**15%**
Bulgur	.5	.5	.5	.5
Couscous			.5	.5
Dried Potatoes	.5	.5	1.0	1.0
Falafel	.5	.5		
Lentils		.5	.5	
Macaroni	2.5	2.5	2.5	2.5
Instant Potatoes		.5	.5	1.0
Refried Beans	.5	.5	.5	.5
Rice	.5	.5	1.0	
Tortillas	1.0	1.0	1.0	1.0
Subtotal	**6.0**	**7.0**	**8.0**	**7.0**
FLOUR				
% OF TOTAL LBS.	**10%**	**10%**	**10%**	**4%**
Basic Batter Mix	1.5	1.5	1.5	1.0
Cornmeal	.5	.5	.5	
Muffin Mix	.5		.5	
Sweet Bread Mix		.5	.5	
Wheat	.5	.5	1.0	
White	.5	.5		1.0
Subtotal	**3.5**	**3.5**	**4.0**	**2.0**
HIGH CALORIE ITEMS (OK HIGH Fat)				
% OF TOTAL LBS.	**13%**	**13%**	**13%**	**18%**
Cheese	2.0	2.0	2.0	3.5
Margarine	1.0	1.0	1.5	2.0
Meats				2.0
Oil	.5	.5	.5	
Peanut Butter	.5	1.0	1.0	
Tahini				.5
Subtotal	**4.0**	**4.5**	**5.0**	**8.0**

MUNCHABLES

% OF TOTAL LBS.	20%	20%	20%	22%
Candy	.5	.5	1.0	1.0
Crackers				.5
Dried Fruit	1.5	1.5	1.5	1.0
Fruit Bars	1.0	.5	1.0	1.0
High Energy Bars	.5	2.0	1.0	2.0
Pita Bread				1.0
Nuts and/or Seeds	1.5	1.5	1.5	1.5
Trail Mix	1.0	1.0	2.0	2.0
Subtotal	**6.0**	**7.0**	**8.0**	**10.0**

DRINKS AND SUGARS

% OF TOTAL LBS.	10%	10%	10%	12%
Brown Sugar	.75	1.0	1.0	1.0
Coffee*				
Fruit Crystals(no Nutrasweet *)	.5	.75	1.0	1.5
Honey				
Hot Chocolate	1.25	1.25	1.5	1.25
Jello (No Nutrasweet*)		.5	.5	1.25
Tea Bags*	20	20	20	20
White Sugar				.5
Subtotal	**2.5**	**3.5**	**4.0**	**5.5**

DESSERTS

% OF TOTAL LBS.	3%	3%	3%	3%
Brownies		.5		.5
Cheesecake			.5	.5
Cake Mix	.5	.5	.5	
Pudding	.5	.25	.5	.5
Subtotal	**1.0**	**1.25**	**1.5**	**1.5**

MISCELLANEOUS

% OF TOTAL LBS.	8%	8%	8%	10%
Bouillon*	yes	yes	yes	yes
Buttermilk		.5	.5	
Cup O Soups	.5	.5	.5	1.0
Dried Vegetables*	yes	yes	yes	yes
Egg Powder	.5	.5	.5	
Instant Soup Mix				.5
Milk	1.25	1.25	1.25	1.75
Miso				
Sauce Mix*	yes	yes	yes	yes
Ramen Soup			.5	.75
Tomato Base	.25	.25	.25	.25
Subtotal	**2.5**	**3.0**	**3.5**	**4.25**

* You want to bring these items but don't count them in your total weight as they add no or very little calories.

trips. It's just so convenient when you crawl into camp exhausted to have a Bag-A-Feast ready to go. You don't have to think. This plan also makes more sense for short trips.

HOW TO DO IT: IMPORTANT DETAILS

NUMBER OF SPECIFIC MEALS: How many breakfasts, lunches and dinners will you need?

TRIP MENU: You will need to decide what you will eat at those specific meals.

NUMBER OF PEOPLE: You will need this to estimate the amount of food needed per meal and some bulk items like drinks, dry milk, oil, etc. As a starting point, one pound of dry ingredients per meal usually satisfies about 3 hungry outdoor types.

FINAL CHECK: We get scared because we're used to Total Ration Planning, so, as a final check, we always weigh our food to see if we're in the correct weight range for the number of people x number of days x number of lbs. per day.

SAMPLE MENU FOR A WEEKEND TRIP

FRIDAY	SATURDAY	SUNDAY
	Breakfast	**Breakfast**
	Granola and milk	Pancakes and syrup
	Dried Fruit	Dried Fruit
	Hot chocolate	International Coffee
	Munchables	**Munchables**
	cheese and crackers	meat and crackers
	fruit bars, gorp	energy bars and gorp
	fruit drink	energy drink
Dinner	**Dinner**	
Tea	Tea	
Curried Rice	Lisagna Lasagna	
Fruit Crunch	Pudding	

CONSIDERATIONS FOR SPECIAL ENVIRONMENTS

If you're trying to save weight and water, freeze-dried foods can usually cut 20% of your total food poundage and save you significant amounts of fuel as well. This can be very helpful in the desert where water is scarce or in winter when you're melting snow for water.

We never go completely freeze-dried, but we occasionally throw some in for special situations like those listed above or high on mountains when you're almost too tired to breathe, never mind cook. Their light weight also makes them great extra food. Forget them in the bottom of your pack until an emergency arises. It's nice to be able to pull them out and just add hot water.

Repackaging and Re-Supplying

OPTION 1: BULK BAGGING

Under the Total Ration Plan we package food in 1-2 pound plastic bags without labeling the bags. It is helpful to have a small scale, but, if you don't, there is a Pounds-to-Cups Chart in the appendix with the most commonly packed foods listed.

If you want to label the bags, go ahead, but it's really only necessary for the "white" dry goods. Even with experience, powdered milk, cheesecake, flour, couscous, grits, baking mix, and potato flakes can start to look alike, especially in the dim light of your head lamp.

We prefer 2 ml plastic bags that you can tie in a loose knot in the top. This works great, but be prepared to assassinate the first person who carries the bag by the knot. After that the knots are never too tight. Some people prefer to use zip-lock bags although we find that they often pop open in your pack if you're not careful to remove the air from the bag and keep the food out of the zip-locking mechanism. It's a good idea to double bag items such as cheese or margarine (even if they're in screw-top containers) because they can leak oil into your pack. Even bouillon cubes will melt in the heat. You can buy a bag-sealing appliance. They work great, but once you re-open the bag it becomes useless.

If the group size gets much above 4-5 people, we plan on cooking in two groups. Otherwise the pressure on the stove is too great and meals start taking longer and longer which, of course, makes your companions grumpier and grumpier. Three to four people per stove is ideal.

OPTION 2: BAG-A-FEAST

This is more time-consuming than bulk bagging, but it will save you a lot of effort in the backcountry. Consult your daily menu and bag all ingredients needed for each individual meal into a single large plastic bag. If all ingredients are not cooked together, small bags may be needed to keep the ingredients separate until you use them. We usually bag breakfasts and dinners, marking them "B" and "D" respectively (some people even number them for the specific day), and then have additional bags marked: drinks, desserts, spices and oil/margarine. Munchables are distributed throughout the group.

Sample Bag-A-Feast: Quick Curried Rice

AT HOME: Put rice, bouillon cube, red and green peppers into a $^1/_2$ gallon sized plastic bag. Put chopped dried fruit, spices, and peppers into a smaller bag and seal. Put nuts and coconut in a smaller bag and seal. Put smaller bags in larger bag and seal.

IN CAMP: Pull out the bag and follow the directions in this book for Quick Curried Rice.

ADDITIONAL HINTS

Most folks can comfortably carry a 8-10 day ration of food. After 10 days the weight starts cutting into the fun, not to mention your hips.

Some folks like to separate their meals into color-coded or marked bags: breakfast bag, lunch bag and dinner bag. This works if a group always travels together, but if you aren't or someone gets separated from their party, they may have to eat dry macaroni elbows for lunch. If it's a paddling trip, we advise you to divide the food types between boats. If one boat goes over and you lose a food bag, you won't lose all the candy bars or all the dinner food. These small things can be the key to a happy expedition.

Make sure you pack your stove and fuel well away from and below the food. A fuel leak is a terrible thing to have on top of your food.

Pack several matchbooks (and a lighter) in different places. If you don't, and they rub together and ignite in your pack, you better hope somebody on your trip is genetically sound enough to have packed some extra matches.

When repackaging cheese try not to touch it (wear gloves or plastic bags on your hands). Also, although recycling is a great thing, use fresh bags for cheese. These two things delay mold process.

RE-SUPPLYING

For most backcountry trips, after approximately 10 days, you will have to rendezvous with your re-supply or go home.

Whatever method of re-supply you choose, make sure the food is packed in weather-proof and animal-proof containers. Package your food so the loss of one container doesn't mean the loss of all of one type of food.

CACHES

Before the trip begins, you can hide a pre-determined amount of food along your route and pick it up later. It's always better if you secure your own cache since somebody else's X on the map easily turns into a cold, hungry treasure hunt with an unhappy end result. It can be very hard to find caches. Completely clean up the cache when you're done. Leaving trash and food in the backcountry is uncool.

Caches are illegal in many National Parks and designated wilderness areas. Call before you cache.

ROADHEADS

Plan your trip in a couple of big circles and re-supply at your car. Or have a friend meet you at a roadhead with your re-supply.

POST OFFICES

Mail yourself your re-supply to a post office along your route. Mail it well in advance with a holding date on the label. Also, many small post offices have limited hours, so be prepared to wait . . . or call first and ask.

COMMERCIAL PACKERS

You can arrange for a commercial packer to deliver your re-supply to you at a given place and time. Prices and weight limits vary. If you're using a commercial re-supplier, make sure you get everything in writing, including the meeting point and time and what will happen if you're late. Having the re-supply dropped indiscriminately means you go hunting for it later. It's not the best plan. The local chamber of commerce closest to the area in which you are traveling can often send you information. Sometimes the National Park Service, USFS, or BLM are helpful.

BOATS AND AIRPLANES

You may be able to arrange re-supply by boat if you are traveling past a major watercourse.

We have been re-supplied by air several times, but it's not cheap and it is illegal in many places, such as most National Parks and designated wilderness areas. The pilots generally prefer to land and hand you your re-supply. This should be your first choice, too. Looking for boxes that landed in the trees is no fun, and sometimes they pop open.

Just Add Water: Freeze-Dried and Dehydrated Food

Freeze-dried food has undergone a unique process that goes something like this: the food, cooked or fresh, gets frozen very solid then placed in freezing temperatures with warm air flowing around it long enough for the moisture to sublimate off. Since ice crystals never form, the cells of the food remain relatively undamaged and most of the nutrition is left intact. 99% plus of the foods water is removed, so the result is very light in weight, and the bulk is reduced a little. And since the cells are undamaged, they hydrate quickly and easily.

Dehydrated food is exposed to low heat in order to drive the water out. Old dehydration methods drove out a lot of nutrition as well. Newer methods preserve much of the nutritional value. A dehydrated product has 90-97% of its water removed. Dehydration shrinks the size of the cells, reducing the weight and bulk a lot, and increasing the time it takes to hydrate the food.

The quality of the hydrated food, whether freeze-dried or dehydrated, depends primarily on the quality of the food before the water was removed. The price of both tends to be high compared to cooking from scratch. Both products offer benefits to the backcountry chef. You can add vegetables and fruits that almost seem fresh to your dishes. You can have a quick, hot meal if you get into camp late. You can combine them with other foods to alter your diet. You can carry a few extra meals in case of an emergency without adding much weight.

FACTS AND FEELINGS ON SOME DRIED FOODS

(See Sources in appendix for ordering information.)

Serving sizes (portions) for freeze-dried/dehydrated meals vary considerably, from 3 ounces (very small) to 14 ounces (large). Most people require somewhere around 12 ounces to feel content. Be aware of serving sizes when you buy.

Adventure Foods: Lots of meals, serving sizes for two or four people. Lots of delicious and easy-to-use mixes prepared especially for the BakePacker. Foods come with

Back Packer directions and regular directions. They offer a cookbook of recipes for the Back packer, too. A selection of individual food and specialty items including vegetables and soybean "meatless meats." Some great soups. Available primarily via mail-order. Cheesy Tuna Casserole tastes like a good cheesy tuna casserole, but it's better with added cheese. Adventure Foods are like real, downhome food. Portions vary from very small to fairly large.

AlpineAire: Very wide variety of no-cooking-required meals, side-dishes, soups and breakfasts. Mostly freeze-dried, some dehydrated. Serving sizes mostly for two people, some meals prepared for four. You can order individual items: meats, vegetables, cheese powder, tomato powder. Quick mail-order service: Ask for the Great Outdoor Chef's Companion, a free catalog. Leonardo da Fettucine is tasty, but left us still hungry. Wild Tyme Turkey hydrated well, but tasted bland. Overall we found AlpineAire needed lots of added spices to satisfy our taste buds. Portions are medium.

Backpacker's Pantry: Many excellent dinners that serve two. Some Complete Meals for four. Lots of breakfasts, desserts, snacks, and individual food items: meats (including jerky), vegetables, fruits and beverages (including very good single-serving coffee bags). Mail-order available. Fast, friendly service. Cheese Pizza tastes like an over-packaged, expensive bagel chip. Santa Fe Chicken is simply the best. Huevos Rancheros very good. Strawberry Cheesecake excellent. We rated Backpacker's Pantry overall best for taste. Portions are medium to large.

Chamy Snacks: They offer more than very tasty, wholesome snacks. Also soups, meats, breads, desserts and unique meals. Change-of-pace foods such as cranberries and sweet bell peppers, chocolate apricots and wild rice soup. Almond Crusader Bar is snack-sized fruit cake, delicious. Portions are small to medium.

Harvest Foodworks: A choice of 12 meals that serve two. Several desserts, breakfasts, and vegetables are available. No meats or meat products are used. Meals come in reusable, reclosable plastic bags that are marked for measuring up to four cups. Combination of freeze-dried and dehydrated foods taking a bit longer to prepare. Oriental Sweet and Sour Dinner took 20 minutes to cook, but the taste was very good. Their eggs taste like real eggs. Harvest Foodworks makes wholesome, good-tasting food that we thought needed added spices. Portions are large and filling.

Mountain House: The only truly all-freeze-dried company. Lots of dinners, breakfasts, snacks and vegetables. Currently offer no vegetarian entrees. No mail-order available, but several mail-order businesses offer Mountain House. Beef Teriyaki hydrated very quickly, tasted good, left us still hungry. Beef Stew hydrated quickly and well, great taste, but we had to eat one each to satisfy our appetites. We rated Mountain House next best for taste. Portions are small to medium.

Richmoor/Natural High: Richmoor for "camping food" and Natural High for "gourmet camping food." Large selection of dinners (some vegetarian), lunches and breakfasts that serve two or four. Complete meals are available. Vegetables, desserts, snacks. Combination of freeze-dried and dehydrated. Honey Lime Chicken was a bit sweet and the chicken didn't quite hydrate in the time they said it would. Chicken Fajitas hydrated easily and well, and the tortilla chips were really crunchy. Portions are medium.

Sorrenti Family Farms: Specializes in very tasty fresh-dried wild rice meals in combination with vegetables or fruits, spices and natural flavorings. No artificial flavorings or preservatives. Ask for the "mini" Quick Gourmet Mixes, packaged for the backcountry. Offers muffin mixes with wild rice flour, and pizza kits. Good wholesome food. Portions small to medium.

Traveling Light: Gourmet baking at its outdoor finest. Mixes, designed especially for their Outback Oven but usable in any baking method, include brownies rich enough to be candy, outstanding pizza, coffee cake, carrot cake, apple pie, nut bread, quiche, corn bread and scones. Just like Mama makes it. Traveling Light also offers handy accessories for their ovens to make outdoor baking less intimidating. Mixes fit 8-10 inch pan. Portions are large.

Uncle John's Foods: Real food air-dried the old fashioned way. Requires the longest of all to prepare (presoaking required), but worth it. All meals 100% vegetarian and serve two. No artificial nothing. A small company offering ten dinners, with provocative names such as Dancing Vegetables and Flying Burritos, and two salads . . . yes, salads. Give Uncle John a try. Mail-order only. Portions are large.

Many pre-cooked freeze-dried and dehydrated outdoor meals can be hydrated right in their package, saving pot cleanup. But the hydrating water-filled packages are hot and squirmy. (We've dumped a couple of meals on the ground.) Be careful and/or carry a PouchMate, a folding plastic hot pouch handler. 3.3 ounces. And they make great desktop letter holders when you're home writing a book.

High Energy Drinks and Bars

THE DRINKS

It used to be that the experts thought water was absorbed by your body faster than high energy drinks. Now they say a high energy drink, one up to about 6% carbohydrate, is actually absorbed faster than water once it reaches the small intestine. Although plain water and a high energy drink will have the same influence on body temperature control, metabolic waste removal, and cardiovascular function in general, high energy drinks provide an energy boost for hard-working muscles. As an added benefit, the drinks give water a sweet taste that encourages consumption. During periods of moderate exercise, you can water down a high energy drink with three or four times the recommended amount of water.

High energy drinks also contain electrolytes, particularly sodium, potassium and chloride, which are necessary to motivate muscles and balance fluids in your body. When you're working hard, some electrolytes, specifically sodium, are lost in your sweat. For most people, a balanced diet replaces all the electrolytes you need. But when the ambient temperature and your exercise level are high, especially when you're not acclimatized to the high heat, you'll benefit from the electrolytes in high energy drinks.

Salt tablets should be considered a curse, and avoided. They are too strong, can irritate your stomach, cause nausea, and increase your body's need for fluid.

FACTS AND FEELINGS ON SOME HIGH ENERGY DRINKS

Today's market offers many high energy drinks. We've used and appreciated these. (See Sources in appendix for ordering information.)

Cytomax: A high energy drink with an additive that helps remove lactic acid from muscles after exercise. You should feel less fatigue and recover faster. Available in packets of 40 grams of powder, with 30 grams being carbohydrate. Suggested serving size: one packet per 16 ounces of water. Three tasty flavors.

E-mergen-C: Energy and electrolytes, plus vitamin C. Handy packets carry one serving. One tangy fruit flavor. Effervescent powder fizzes in your water bottle. If water is low, you can dump the contents straight into your mouth, but be prepared to pucker. We've downed a lot of this one.

Exceed: 7.2 % carbohydrate. Two pleasant fruity flavors. Available in a small pouch— pour all the contents into your water bottle—or a larger sturdy pouch from which you can pour out the amount you want.

Gatorade: The original high energy drink. Lots of flavors that we like. 6% carbohy- drate. Available as Gatorade Light at 2.5% carbohydrate. Available in durable packets that pack well and mix easily. Also available in bulk containers.

Sqwincher: 6.8% carbohydrate. Several fine-tasting flavors. Available in instant dry mix that packs well and mixes easily. Available in liquid concentrate packets to which you just add water and drink from the package.

THE BARS

Once upon a time, not long ago, there was only PowerBar. Now the market shelves bend under the load of nearly two dozen rivals in the energy bar industry. If you're fac- ing a long day or when you just want a power-up snack, energy bars can provide a healthy boost. Whatever brand you choose, choose carefully. Energy bars should be no more than 25%, or near that, fat. Make sure the bulk of the carbohydrates are complex (rice, oats, glucose polymers, maltodextrin for example) for staying power, and not simple sugars.

If you're anticipating a long haul, eat a bar before you get going in order to stoke the fires of your engine. If you're pooped at the end of the long haul, eat one to restore your energy. If you need a boost, say every hour or so, take a bite of bar. And remem- ber energy bars need lots of water to work, so drink regularly and often.

FACTS AND FEELINGS ON SOME ENERGY BARS

With so many bars to choose from, you'll probably want to try several to find your favorite. Nobody feels the same about the same bar. Any of these will probably do the job. (See Sources in appendix for ordering information.)

Clif Bars: 80% carbohydrate, low-fat. Four flavors including Double Chocolate. Taste is OK. Easy to chew. Fairly large size, but they don't seem as filling to us as PowerBars.

Cytobar: 72% carbohydrate, low-fat. Couple of flavors. One of us liked the taste a lot, especially the Jazzberry, and other one didn't. Very easy to chew.

Edgebar: 75% carbohydrate, low-fat. Chocolate. Good taste, though a bit dry, with a peculiar aftertaste. Not too hard on the teeth.

Exceed Sports Bar: 76% carbohydrate, very low-fat. Chocolate only. Very good taste. Takes some chewing to get it down. If it isn't our favorite, it's very close.

FinHalsa: 66% carbohydrate, low-fat. Raisin Nut Crunch, Raspberry and Chocolate Mousse. Good taste, almost like candy. Easier on the teeth than most energy bars. Small size makes you want more. One of our favorites.

PowerBar: The original energy bar and an old favorite. 71% carbohydrate, very low-fat. Several flavors, and the new crunchier (but still very chewy) bars taste better than the old ones. We've eaten a lot of these, and like Malt-Nut and Apple Crisp best.

PurePower: 70% carbohydrate, low-fat. Chocolate, Peanut and Mountain Berry flavors with good taste. On the chewy side.

Tiger Sport: 71% carbohydrate, low-fat. Several flavors offer OK taste, though kind of sweet. Fairly easy to chew.

THE BACKCOUNTRY KITCHEN

Setting Up the Outdoor Kitchen

AN ENVIRONMENTAL PERSPECTIVE

Within sixty easy paces, from one end of the clearing to the other, four old fire-rings of blackened rocks surrounding mounds of ash, nearby earth compacted into the consistency of concrete, stand as ugly reminders that camp kitchens may remain to scar the backcountry long after you're history. Not an uncommon sight, but an outdoor kitchen *today* should have as little impact on the environment as possible.

Your environmental kitchen ideally sits in a comfortable spot, protected from unappealing weather conditions, offering an inspiring view. It should also be, ideally, an isolated spot where you aren't an uninspiring view to other backcountry users. And it should be durable, a place that has the best chance to be impacted the least.

The greatest impact of kitchens, and to the backcountry in general, comes from destruction of vegetation and compaction of the soil, with the common result of erosion. Intensity of use determines much of a kitchen's impact (how many people have sat, stood and walked around there before), but your behavior and your choice of sites will also affect your ability to leave no trace.

Concerning intensity, a heavily used spot, which means a campsite utilized more than 10 times (according to the US Forest Service), does not significantly deteriorate with further use. Most of the impact comes in the first one or two times a site is used improperly. That means if you have a choice between an obviously impacted spot and a nearby pristine spot, you'll do far less damage settling where the damage has already been done. But leave it as pretty as possible. In high use areas, you want to encourage other people to use the same site instead of creating a new one.

If you're using an unspoiled spot, choosing the cooking site ranks as the single most important consideration in terms of an environmental kitchen. First, start looking for the best site early, before fatigue or darkness urges you to drop down in the most convenient space. If the site shows evidence of previous use, don't cook there. The most ideal spots are without vegetation, or even soil: sand, rocks, gravel, snow. Second best are soil-based sites without vegetation. Even though your stay will cause some compaction, recovery is rapid. If you have to choose between dense vegetation and sparse vegetation, go for the dense. Sparse plant life disturbs easier than a thick carpet of vegetation. Wet grass and dewy flowers die easily when trampled. Low shrubs and baby trees take a long time to come back from abuse. Marshy ground recovers slowly from heavy use. Dense dry grass, on the other hand, or under the other foot, makes a tough durable surface. An open meadow of grass, even though you'll be more visible to other campers, recovers quicker than thin vegetation hidden under a forest canopy. In short, don't rearrange the earth to suit you, find a spot on it that suits it and you.

Your behavior requires more attention to details. Large parties, groups of more than four or five, leave less impact if they break into smaller kitchen groups. This is especially true in more pristine areas. Wearing soft-soled shoes around the kitchen mars the land less than boots. Reduce your movement around the kitchen as much as possible, especially in vegetated spots. Avoid making trails. Walking back and forth from tent to stove along the same path several times may leave a track noticeable for years. Minimize your stay in one place. It's best for the land to move every day.

When it's time to move on, check one more time to make sure you're packing out everything you packed in. Look for spillage at the cooking site, flour or rice that puffed out during mixing, food that fell off the plate during eating in the dark. Fluff up grass or other vegetation that got pressed down. Sprinkle duff or other natural materials over marred areas. Replace rocks or logs you may have rolled out of the way. Use a dead branch to sweep away even your tracks.

PREP AREA VS. COOK AREA

When you plan a lot of mixing and stirring, establish a food preparation area apart from the cooking area. This will prevent the problem of having to start a pot of water toward boiling a second time because you knocked the first pot over.

SAFE FOOD STORAGE

Improper storage of camp food can attract unwelcome visitors: the small ones that might eat your food, and the big ones that might eat you. Since your cooking area will be well away from your sleeping area, keeping all food in the cooking area concentrates odors in one relatively safe spot. We carry food double-bagged in plastic in a zippered duffel bag to reduce odor even more. Odorous garbage stays in the food storage bag, in its own separate bag. If the chance of a bear encounter is minimal, you can leave the food on the ground or, preferably, hang it casually from the limb of a tree. If bears frequent the area, better hang the food high. The most bear-proof hanging method requires the food bag be suspended between two trees, a minimum of 12 feet off the ground and a minimum of 12 feet from each tree. This is a laborious process, but we've used it where bear populations are dense. You can usually get by hauling the food bag up about 12 feet off the ground from a limb. A new contraption, an unbreakable bear-proof plastic container, guarantees your food will be safe. It might be worth the money and weight if bears are thick and trees are not.

QUICK SUMMARY

1. Minimize environmental damage.
2. Minimize visual contact with other folks.
3. Maximize protection from unwelcome weather.
4. Maximize protection from unwelcome pests.
5. Maximize view.

Stoves and Fuel

Beneath every delicious one-burner meal you'll find, at some point, a one-burner stove. Your choice of stoves will help determine the outcome of meal preparation . . . and your level of frustration during cooking. Although you may not find one ideal stove for all occasions, these general tips should help you make your choice.

1. **Weight and Size.** Some excellent stoves weigh far too much and take up too much room to be practical in the wilderness. Happy cooks choose a stove that packs easily and weighs in between a pound and a pound and a half when empty of fuel.

2. **Heat Output Intensity and Range.** The more intense the heat, measured in BTUs, the less time it takes to boil water. Efficient stoves will boil a quart of water in less than five minutes. But intense heat is not something you'll want all the time. Chefs need to be able to turn the heat down in order to simmer some fine meals.

3. **Ease of Operation.** A stove that starts easily and handles easily, even in cold weather, is the stove you want.

4. **Stability.** Stoves that wobble when you set a pot on the burner are likely to dump your well-earned gourmet meal in the dirt. Choose a stove with a stable base, one that has an adequate pot support surface and a relatively low profile.

5. **Windscreens.** Wind reduces the efficiency of your stove. Wind can snuff out the flame when you need it most. You can't control the wind, but you can choose a stove with a windscreen . . . or one for which you can make a windscreen.

6. **Durability.** Packs with stoves stuffed inside get dropped, sat on, stuffed into trunks of cars, and banged against trees. Choose a stove that can withstand the punishment.

7. **Accessories.** Some stoves come with a fuel bottle. That's nice. Some stoves come with a stuff sack. That's nice, too . . . protective sacks add to the life expectancy of your stove. Some stoves come with repair kits. Another nice option. You don't want to be far from home without a stove repair kit.

8. **Fuel Used.** In the United States, any fuel you want is available. In many foreign countries, fuel types are limited. Make sure your stove will utilize the fuel you'll have available.

9. **Cost.** The amount you pay does not necessarily indicate the efficiency of the stove for your purposes. Choose the stove that will work best, and then decide how to pay for it.

STOVE FUELS

Alcohol. Heat output is low. Flammability is high. Burns clean and spills evaporate quickly without leaving a harmful residue.

Automotive Gasoline. Use unleaded only. Leaded gas produces toxic fumes when burned. Explosions are possible. Heat output is high. Flammability is also high. Stoves may clog with prolonged use.

Butane. Must be carried in cartridges. Burns clean. Most cartridges can't be changed until they're empty and heat output goes down as fuel runs low. Easy and safe to use. Heat output is reduced by cold temperatures. Must be kept above freezing.

Butane/Propane Mix. Must be carried in cartridges. Burns clean. Easy and safe to use. Performs well at high altitude and in cold temperatures.

Kerosene. Heat output high. Flammability lowest of all fuels, but it smells. If you spill some it remains oily unlike other fuels that evaporate quickly.

Propane. Must be carried in cartridges. Burns clean. Easy and safe to use. Performs well in cold.

White Gas (or naphtha). Heat output is high. Flammability is high and explosions are possible. Burns clean. Much cheaper than cartridges of fuel. Works well at high altitude. Works well in cold although pre-heating burner might be required.

TIPS FOR FIGURING LIQUID FUEL NEEDS

On Summer trips, figure $1/6$ quart per person per day. That's $3/6$ or $1/2$ quart per person for a three day trip. One quart per person for a six day trip.

On Fall and Spring trips, figure $1/4$ quart per person per day, especially if you're traveling in a cold climate and/or at higher altitudes.

On Winter trips and at High Altitude, figure $1/2$ quart per person per day, especially if you're melting snow for water. Better safe than sorry.

STOVE SAFETY AND MAINTENANCE TIPS

1. Keep your stove covered when you're not using it. Carry it in a stuff sack or kit. Keeping dirt and dust out of your stove prolongs its life and reduces maintenance.

2. Be sure your gas stove is cool before refilling. Refill outside your tent and well away from other heat sources. Use a funnel or a fuel bottle-cap with a built-in pour spout to avoid spillage when refueling.

3. Fill stoves and fuel bottles that attach to stoves no more than two-thirds to three-fourths full in order to maintain air space for pressure.

4. If fuel spills on the stove during filling, allow it to evaporate before lighting.

5. If you melt snow for water, plan on at least two quarts per person per week.

6. Using a cover on pots while cooking reduces the amount of fuel you'll use.

7. Carry and store stoves and fuel well separated from foods.

8. Carry fuel in containers made for carrying fuel.

9. Do NOT burn automotive gasoline in a tent or snow cave or any enclosed area. If you must cook inside a tent or snowcave, with fuel other than auto gas, light the stove outside the enclosed area, then move it inside. Make sure adequate ventilation is maintained at all times.

10. Try new stoves in your backyard before heading out on the long trail.

11. Practice taking your stove apart at home in case you have to repair it in the field.

12. Carry a stove repair kit.

FACTS AND FEELINGS ON SOME STOVES

(See Sources in the appendix for ordering information.)

BIBLER

Hanging Stove. Innovative, this stove hangs from anything convenient, including the inside of your tent, if you're careful and provide adequate ventilation. Weighs in at 29 ounces which includes the two-quart pot, lid and handle. Great stability when hanging. Windscreen/heat reflector envelopes the pot and burner for efficiency. Easy to use. Requires a butane/propane cartridge.

CAMPING GAZ

Rando 360. Very compact. Comes with two pots, windscreen, pot clamp and strap that nest together tidily. Weight without cartridge 22 ounces. Low profile makes stability good. Uses a butane cartridge that burns about one hour at full strength. Takes longer than many stoves to boil a quart of water. Not good for group cooking.

SOME
PACKING
STOVES

PEAK ·1

S470

ULTRA 470

MSR XGK

Ultra 470. Super-sized butane/propane cartridge burns about four and a half hours. Stove screws into top of cartridge. Boils a quart of water in under five minutes. Weight with cartridge 41 ounces. Automatic ignition. Stable when base ring is used.

COLEMAN

The Coleman Company, long a leader in outdoor stoves, has several excellent one-burners, including:

Peak 1 Apex and Apex II. Pump fits into fuel bottle, connected to stove via a flexible hose. Weighs in at 18.6 ounces. High heat output with great simmering ability. Easy to use. Low profile for stability. Apex uses white gas. Apex II uses white gas or unleaded gasoline. Both are adaptable to kerosene.

Peak 1 Feather 442 Dual Fuel. One-piece stove. Weighs 23.25 ounces. High heat output, simmers great. Easy to use. Fold out-legs provide good stability. Packs neatly in padded stuff sack (sold separately). Windscreen available. Uses white gas or unleaded gasoline. One of our favorites.

Peak 1 Multi-Fuel: Like a smaller Feather 442. Weighs 20.8 ounces. High heat output, simmers just fine. Easy to use. Burns white gas or adapts to kerosene.

EPIgas

EPIgas Back-Packing Stove. Made in England, EPIgas stoves burn butane/propane from a cartridge that seals snugly for safety. Three cartridge sizes are available. Stove is lightweight and packs well. Easy to use with adjustable flame control. Stability good when used with stabilizer base. Windscreen available. Appliance weight without windscreen approximately 7 ounces.

EPIgas Picnic Stove. Similar to Back-Packing Stove with built in windscreen making it a little heavier. Burns a bit hotter so it's better at higher altitudes and lower temperatures. Both stoves are available with an automatic lighting mechanism. Weight approximately 11 ounces.

EPIgas Alpine Stove. Low profile for greater stability. Takes a little bit longer to boil water. Weight approximately 12 ounces.

MOUNTAIN SAFETY RESEARCH

MSR XGK II. It's been around a long time, and it's proven its worth. Burns almost any fuel. When the temperature plunges and the altitude soars, the XGK II delivers high heat. No one-burner boils water faster. Excellent for mountaineering. Fairly easy to use. Priming required. Pump fits in fuel bottle and connects to stove via rigid tube. Kind of awkward to pack safely and a bit tippy on rough terrain. Noisy. Does not simmer. Weighs in at 15.5 ounces with fuel pump, windscreen, heat reflector and stuff sack. Our favorite at high altitude.

MSR WhisperLite. Easy to use, works well in cold . . . and quiet, as the name implies. Produces intense heat but adjusts to simmer a meal as well. Folds up to pack neatly inside many pots. More stable than the XGK II. Burns white gas only. Weighs in at 13.5 ounces with fuel pump, windscreen, heat reflector, and stuff sack.

MSR WhisperLite Internationale. Very much like the WhisperLite but it also burns kerosene. Same weight, same accessories.

RapidFire. Simple to use. Variable flame control. Burns isobutane fuel from cartridge. Cartridge may be removed from stove for easier packing. Weight with windscreen, heat reflector and stuff sack 12.5 ounces.

OPTIMUS

Optimus 111 Hiker. Stable, must be primed, works well in wind and cold. Unit folds up into heavy, but very durable 7x7 box. Weighs in at 54 ounces. Adjustable intensity, with great simmering ability. Burns white gas, kerosene or alcohol. A proven performer in the arena of one-burners. One of our favorites.

Optimus 123R Climber (Svea). Compact and durable, a bit tippy, works well at higher altitudes but performs less well in cold. Must be primed. Burns white gas only. Loses efficiency without windscreen. Weighs in at 19.5 ounces.

PRIMUS

Primus 2243. Made in Sweden, Primus stoves use a butane/propane cartridge. Heat output is high, and flame is easily adjusted. Built-in wind baffle for more efficiency. Packs easily. Fairly stable with addition of cartridge support. Additional Power Booster transfers heat from burner to cartridge for more efficiency in cold. Automatic ignition available. Appliance weighs about 9 ounces.

Primus 2263. Similar to 2243 but less efficient. No wind baffle. Appliance weight about 4.5 ounces.

Primus 3263. Similar to 2263 but comes with automatic ignition. Appliance weight about 7 ounces.

Primus 3233. Stable spider-like stove with cartridge attached by hose. Heat output high. Packs small. Automatic ignition. Appliance weight about 13 ounces.

SIGG

Fire-Jet. Made in Switzerland, this new (and untested) multi-fuel stove has hinged supports that offer considerable stability and fold up for easy packing. Flexible tube connects pump, which fits into fuel bottles, to the stove. Weight with pump 10.75 ounces.

YOUR STOVE IN THE COLD OUTDOORS

When it gets really cold, neither you nor your stove are going to function optimally. Some stoves will require preheating. Some stoves won't work at all, especially some of the cartridge types. If you plan to cook outside in winter conditions, make sure you know your stoves capabilities.

YOUR STOVE AT HIGH ALTITUDE

When you go up in altitude, the amount of oxygen you and your stove take in with each breath goes down. At 18,000 feet the oxygen in the ambient air is only about one-half what it is at sea level. That means the efficiency of your stove goes down. If there's not enough oxygen for your stove to burn all the fuel being released, the flame will be cooler and yellower. If you plan to go high, make sure you know your stoves capabilities.

And remember water boils at a lower temperature the higher you go. That adds to inefficiency, also. So it takes longer to cook food at altitude, which means you'll need more fuel. Plan accordingly.

Gear for the Outdoor Kitchen

As every cook and carpenter know, one of the big secrets of a great product is using the right tool for the job. In the backcountry, gourmet meals can be prepared with a minimum of simple cookgear, but it should be thoughtfully chosen for maximum chef-ness. (See Sources in the appendix for ordering information.)

POTS AND PANS

Stainless steel pots cost more and weigh a little more, but they hold up better under outdoor abuse, and they're a bit easier to clean. They conduct heat a little slower than aluminum. Some outdoor stainless steel pots have copper on the bottom to increase heat conductivity. We prefer stainless steel.

We've read those stories about how *aluminum* flakes off into food, but not enough would ever flake off your outdoor pots to cause a health problem. Aluminum is a good choice: it's light, it's inexpensive, it's available, it works.

Enamel cookware, although functional and colorful, chips and rusts too easily for our use. It is quite safe to use outdoors, the metals under enamel being inert, which means they won't affect your health if you swallow some.

Non-stick coatings, such as Teflon, on pots and pans are made from inert materials. If you choose a non-stick coating for your outdoor cookware, don't worry about chips and don't worry about the coating when it rubs off in spots. Chips will pass harmlessly through your digestive tract, if you swallow one, and there's no health reason to discard pots and pans with worn surfaces.

Depending on the length of trip and number of people, you'll probably want to own a set of pots ranging in size from one to four quarts. You'll decide what you need and carry those pots you'll need to do the job for a particular trip. Even when it's just the two of us, we carry two pots: one to boil water and one to cook in, or one to mix in and one to cook in. Buy sets that nest together for packability. Some people prefer pots with handles, but we find the handles get so hot that we end up using potgrips anyway. It is important that all pots have a lid that fits well. Lids make cooking faster, hold in heat while you're waiting, and reduce the amount of pine needles and grit in your food. Make sure you choose pots with a very limited number of plastic parts.

One pan of approximately 10 inches diameter, the deeper the better (say two inches), with a non-stick surface, is a must for fine cooking. Choose one with a lid. Once again, some people like pans with a folding handle, but we use potgrips for a handleless pan, too. Our favorite is the Banks Fry-Bake Pan, an aluminum pan with an anodized hardcoat for easy cleaning and great durability. The snug-fitting lid allows you to build a twiggy fire on top if baking requires one. It is only available via mail-order.

Pressure cookers can cut cooking time for things like beans almost in half. For high altitude trips, they'll save lots of time and fuel. We don't know of a source of pressure cookers designed especially for outdoor use. Small models are available but very hard to find.

Coffee percolators just right for one-burner stoves, even mini espresso makers, are available from several manufacturers. Coffee connoisseurs will want the extra weight and bulk, but good old "cowboy coffee" can still be made in any old pot.

OUTBACK OVEN

For easy, high-quality baking on a one-burner stove, nothing beats the Outback Oven from Traveling Light. It's not totally foolproof, but a little practice and you'll turn out fabulous breads, pizza and desserts. The Outback Oven Ultralight includes a diffuser plate and riser bars to create hot air out of your stoves energy, a fabric convection dome to trap the hot air around your 6-8 inch pan or pot, and a thermometer to monitor baking temperatures. Outback Oven Plus Ten is a larger version of the Ultralight that comes with a 10-inch pan and lid. An optional aluminum Tutu, an adjustable windscreen, directs heat up the sides of your pot while shielding it from the wind. Traveling Light offers a line of food mixes prepared especially for the Outback Oven.

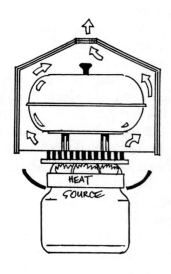

BAKEPACKER

For the ultimate in simple baking, try the Bakepacker from Strike 2 Industries. You just put mixed ingredients in a plastic, yes, plastic bag, place the bag in your pot on top of the Bakepacker, make sure enough water has been added to the pot to cover the cells of the oven, and boil. Because the food is steam-baked you don't get crusty tops, but the system works, and messy post-baking clean-up is eliminated. Adventure Foods sells mixes prepared especially for the Bakepacker.

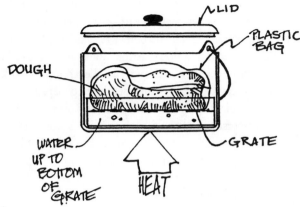

KITCHEN ACCESSORIES

You'll probably be sorry if you don't have a large spoon to serve and stir with, and a spatula. Potgrips are useful, but we carry a small survival tool (Leatherman) which has pliers that work as potgrips, a knife, can opener, and other often-handy attachments. You'll need some plastic containers in various sizes for things such as butter or cooking oil, and spices. Be warned that the Environmental Protection Agency (EPA) advises not using 35mm plastic film canisters for foodstuffs since the plasticizers may rub off into your food. Leftover plastic containers that once contained butter, etc., work, but sometimes they pop open in your pack. We generally prefer containers with screw-on tops. (Hint: If you have small spice/salt/pepper containers with screw-on tops, measure how much the top holds in order to use that measurement later.) Optional items

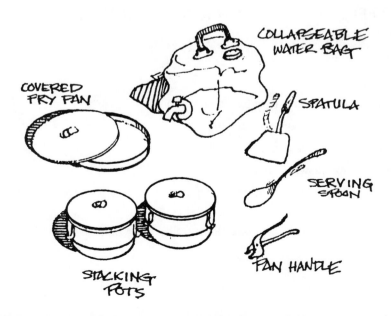

include a small wire whisk, a measuring cup, an abrasive pad for clean-up, and large collapsible water container to keep water readily available in the kitchen.

Much of the frenetic bother of searching for smaller kitchen items can be eliminated by purchasing one of several kitchen-organizer kits. Atwater Carey, Ltd., offers the Campside Kitchen with two each Lexan knives, forks and spoons, a serving spoon, a whisk, can opener, spatula, scrubber, collapsible paper measuring cup and nine containers of various sizes for spices and such. Mesh pockets with lots of room let you carry personal additions. We prefer the Campside Jr.—a smaller version with ample room for gear for two. Outdoor Research Outdoor Kitchens, Compact and Deluxe models, offer the same conveniences.

PERSONAL ITEMS

Everyone needs their personal mug, and we prefer the plastic insulated travel variety, 12-16 ounces, with snap-on lid. Drinks in metal cups seem to always be too hot or too cold. When you know the capacity, they can be used as a guestimater for measuring. To reduce the guesswork, mark your travel mug before your trip. You see these mugs for sale everywhere. Your personal water bottle can be purchased with measuring grids pre-marked by the manufacturer.

A personal bowl is needed when a group travels together. When it's just the two of us, we often eat out of the pots and pans. An unbreakable plastic spoon is needed for eating...unless you want to carve some chopsticks, which we've done when somehow the spoons got left at home. (Hint: If you measure your spoon to see how much it holds, you might find that measurement useful later.) We've never found a need for forks.

OUR PERSONAL OUTDOOR KITCHEN GEAR CHECKLIST:

- ☐ Personal cup
- ☐ Personal bowl
- ☐ Personal spoon
- ☐ Leatherman (for knife, potgrips, can opener)
- ☐ One-quart and two-quart pots with lids
- ☐ Banks Fry-Bake Pan with lid
- ☐ Large collapsible water container
- ☐ Atwater Carey Campside Jr. (with small containers, spatula, large spoon, wire whisk, scrubbing pad)
- ☐ Traveling Light's large convection dome (called a Pot Parka)

Camp Kitchen Hygiene

A CLEAN KITCHEN IS A HEALTHY KITCHEN

Germs (bacteria, viruses, parasites) are responsible for illnesses including yucky stomachs and the early retirement of more backcountry chefs than all other reasons combined. Many germs commonly lurk in backcountry water. Others proliferate in food that's been improperly cooked or stored.

Some germs live long happy lives on human skin, even healthy humans, without bothering those people. But when some of those same germs fall off into breakfast, lunch or dinner preparations, they multiply with great speed and lead to disease. Unhealthy people carry germs that can often be passed easily by hand and mouth. And, disgusting but true, humans have germs living in their bowels, and they share those germs in the camp kitchen when they fail to adequately wash their hands after a bowel movement.

HAND WASHING

All good cooks have at least one thing in common: clean hands. Your outer layer of skin is an overlapping armor of dead cells that protect the living cells beneath. Under a microscope, this outer layer looks like the surface of the Colorado Plateau from thirty thousand feet: canyons and mesas, cracks and fissures. Resident microbes are wedged firmly into the low spots. Some of these microbes are friendly, serving to keep skin slightly acid and resistant to other microbial lifeforms such as fungi. Others can make you severely sick. In addition to the residents, transient germs come and go as fortune dictates. They can accumulate rapidly after bowel movements, and they congregate most thickly under fingernails and in the deeper fissures of fingertips. That's why human hands account for twenty-five to forty percent of all foodborne illness.

Hand washing prior to food handling, even with detergents, does not remove all the flora, but it does significantly reduce the chance of contamination. For your information, science recommends the following eight-step hand washing technique for maximum cleanliness:

1. Wet hands with hot flowing water (100-120 degrees F).

2. Soap up until a good lather is attained.

3. Work the lather all over the surface of the hand concentrating on fingernails and tips.

4. Clean under fingernails.

5. Rinse thoroughly with hot water (very important).

6. Re-soap and re-lather.

7. Re-rinse.

8. Dry with a paper towel (very important) to wipe off bacteria clinging to the water.

For most of us, hot water is a rare wilderness commodity. But you can still get clean hands with this modified backcountry technique which substitutes germicidal soap for hot water. In tests, adequate hand sanitation was achieved with as little as one half-liter of water. Move at least 200 feet away from the source of water when using any soap in the wilderness.

1. Wet hands thoroughly.

2. Add a small amount of germicidal soap (such as Klenzade® or Betadine Scrub® or Hibiclens®).

3. Work lather up, especially fingertips.

4. Clean under fingernails (and keep your nails trimmed).

5. Rinse thoroughly.

6. Repeat soap, lather and rinse.

7. Dry, with a small clean towel or bandanna.

Sure, it's a bother . . . but so is getting sick. And even plain old hand washing beats no hand washing.

FOOD HANDLING

Wilderness food usually shows up in plastic bags, and food contamination can be further reduced by pouring the food out instead of reaching in for it. It ought to go without saying, but here it is anyway: already-sick people should stay out of the kitchen.

Some well-cooked backcountry food doesn't get the opportunity to be processed by the human digestive system. This results from cooking more than you can eat, which is a result, most often, of less than maximum meal planning skills. Storage of cooked-but-uneaten food in the wilderness poses an almost insurmountable problem. Bacteria grows optimally at temperatures ranging from forty-five to ninety degrees Fahrenheit, and unhealthy populations of bacteria can be reached in a brief period of time. A tuna sandwich on a warm day can become dangerous in less than four hours. Reheating cooked food, although it kills bacteria, often leaves dangerous toxins produced by the bacteria at sickening levels. Your safest bet is to not eat leftovers.

Food waiting to be cooked and waiting to be eaten should be covered in the presence of flies and other germ-toting creatures of the air and ground. Food should be stored out of reach of those same creatures.

COOKGEAR AND KITCHEN UTENSILS

Another major source of food contamination in the wilderness is dirty cookwear and kitchen utensils. Your choice of cookwear, say aluminum vs. stainless steel, and utensils, say wood vs. plastic, is irrelevant in terms of germs, but cookwear should be washed and dried daily, and utensils should be cleaned prior to use in the preparation and serving of food. An exception would be extremely cold conditions where food residue freezes before you can wash it off.

PACK IT IN, PACK IT OUT

As any sanitation engineer can tell you, much can be learned about a person by going through their garbage. Same goes for backcountry trash and, in the plus column, the amount of litter has steadily decreased in wilderness areas over the last twenty years despite an increase in litter bearers. But the potential impact of trash ranks low as a health hazard, while the disposition of leftover food and, far more important, human waste products rank as the greatest risk.

WHAT TO DO WITH YOUR DOO

You can't realistically pack out everything you pack in, except in special circumstances (such as dragging frozen feces off of winter trips), but you can, with an adequate poo-poo plan, reduce the risk of fecal contamination to an absolute minimum. Transmission of fecalborne pathogens occurs in four ways: direct contact with the feces (even using toilet paper leaves germs on your hands), indirect contact with hands that have directly contacted the feces, contact with insects that have contacted the feces, and drinking water contaminated with feces.

Human waste products break down to a harmless state as a result of two mechanisms: 1) bacterial action in the presence of oxygen, moisture and warmth, and 2) inactivation from direct ultraviolet radiation and dryness. Deposition of solid body wastes should include placement A) to maximize decomposition, B) to minimize the chance of something or someone finding it, and C) to minimize the chance of water contamination. And, after the deed, wash your hands.

Latrines are out, except in established spots. They concentrate too much poop in one place. They carry a high risk of water pollution. They invite insect and mammal investigation. They are unsightly, and they stink. If you are ever required to dig a latrine, make it at least a foot deep, and add soil after each deposit, and fill it in when the total excreta lies several inches below the surface.

For years, environment- and health-concerned wildland managers have recommended catholes as the best way to manage human feces. Preferably in a level spot, a cathole should be dug several inches into an organic layer of soil, where decomposing microorganisms live most abundantly. After you've dropped your droppings, stir them into the soil to speed decomposition. Cover the mess with a couple of inches of soil, and disguise the spot to hide it from later passersby.

Now it's generally considered that your personal excrement will rot to harmlessness quickest if you use the smear technique, smearing or scattering your dung over the surface to maximize sun and air exposure. Smears (and all human wastes) should be at least two hundred feet, or approximately seventy adult paces, from water and your kitchen, and placed where little chance of discovery exists.

The smear technique has obvious drawbacks in well-used areas where, for one thing, waste won't decompose fast enough to eliminate health hazards. In those places it remains best to defecate in thoughtfully situated catholes.

Although urine contains, normally, an insignificant number of bacteria, it can carry, almost always in developing countries, parasites such as schistosomes. To stay on the safe side, urinate on rocks or in non-vegetated spots far from water sources and your kitchen whenever possible. Urine on the rocks keeps animals from creating an unsightly excavation later.

CARE, BUT DON'T AWAYS SHARE

Nice people are willing to share, but they may be passing around more than their water bottle. Keep your lip balm and your toothbrush to yourself. Personal eating utensils and mugs should stay personal. If you can't finish your candy bar or your lunch, dispose of the leftovers properly instead of passing your germs to someone else.

WATER DISINFECTION

Many invisible bacteria, viruses and parasites find a home in water, and all wilderness water sources should be eyed with suspicion in relation to health. It's not the visible stuff in water that makes you sick, but water with a lot of sediment in it should be strained. You can strain it through anything that will let water pass while trapping the sediment: bandanna, T-shirt, paper coffee filter. But good camp kitchen hygiene requires safe water, and there are still, basically, three ways to insure the quality of water.

1. HEAT

Killing all the microorganisms in water, a process known as sterilization, requires five to ten minutes of boiling at sea level. But not all microorganisms cause illness. Take heat-resistant bacterial spores. They're harmless. Pasteurization, the process of bringing a liquid to almost boiling, works toward killing everything in water that can make a human sick. Giardia dies in 2-3 minutes at 158 degrees F. Viruses die in seconds at 176 degrees F. By the time water reaches the boiling point, worldwide, it's safe to drink, even at an altitude of 19,000 feet where the boiling point of water is 178 degrees F. Water used to cook with does not have to be disinfected prior to use. The cooking process will disinfect it.

2. HALOGENATION

Iodine and chlorine are the best chemical water disinfectants. When used properly, they'll kill most parasites, viruses and bacteria. The effectiveness of halogens depends on their concentration in the water and the amount of time you wait before drinking. In other words, you can reduce the amount of halogen if you're willing to wait longer for it to work. Cold water slows the effect of chemical disinfectants. In cold water, you should use more or wait longer. When opting for halogen use, the safest approach is buying a commercial product and following the instructions. If you're carrying chemical disinfectants, use them in all your drinking water and wait until they have acted before adding anything to the water to sweeten or flavor it.

3. FILTRATION

Many backcountry water filters remove protozoan lifeforms and bacteria, but none will remove viruses. Some filters kill viruses via contact with an iodine resin on the filter. Read the label carefully before buying. Most wilderness water in the United States stands or runs free of harmful viruses. Not so in many foreign countries. If you're carrying a filter, use it to disinfect all drinking water before consumption.

FACTS AND FEELINGS ON SOME WATER FILTERS

(See Sources in the appendix for ordering information.)

First Need Deluxe Water Purifier: Resin/carbon matrix filter. Fairly lightweight, good quality. Awkward to use—takes both hands and feet to operate. Prefilter strains out large debris. Filters strain out parasites and bacteria. Viruses can get through. Carbon within the filter absorbs pesticides, herbicides, solvents, odors and bad tastes. When filter clogs, can be backwashed in the field, but it's not a simple procedure. Pumping requires little effort. Relatively inexpensive.

Katadyn Pocket Filter: Ceramic filter. Dependable, durable, precisely manufactured Swiss product, the look and feel of a fine tool. Prefilter strains out large debris. Filter strains out parasites and bacteria. Does strain out viruses, chemical pollutants, bad tastes or offensive odors. Pumping requires a lot of effort. Requires frequent cleaning, but can be cleaned easily in the field. Very expensive. Katadyn's Mini Filter is a smaller version.

MSR WaterWorks: Carbon block plus membrane filter. Innovative, high quality. Prefilter strains out large debris. Parasites and bacteria are strained out. Viruses can get through. Carbon absorbs chemicals and particles that smell or taste bad. Long lever makes it easy to pump. Can be cleaned in the field, but it's a complex process. Fairly expensive.

PUR Explorer: Membrane with iodine resin filter. Truly innovative, high quality. Prefilter strains out big stuff. Filter strains out parasites and bacteria. Iodine resin kills viruses. Add-on carbon filter removes tastes and smells. Easy to use. Easy to clean in the field. One of our favorites. Fairly expensive. PUR's Scout is a smaller version, clogs much easier, more difficult to clean.

SweetWater Guardian: Stainless steel screen and depth filter. A new step forward in innovation. Prefilter for the big chunks. Screen and depth filter keeps out parasites and bacteria. Add-in Biocide Cartridge guarantees death of everything bad for you, including viruses. Lightweight, easy to clean. Easiest of all to pump. A great favorite. Relatively inexpensive.

Timberline: Lightweight, convenient. Filters out parasites only. Straw-like attachment allows you to suck water right out of the source if you choose. Clogs quickly in sediment-rich water. Cannot be cleaned in the field. Easy to use. Inexpensive.

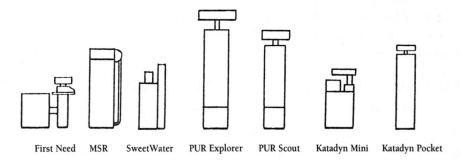

First Need   MSR   SweetWater   PUR Explorer   PUR Scout   Katadyn Mini   Katadyn Pocket

QUICK SUMMARY

1. Keep your hands clean.
2. Don't save leftovers overnight.
3. Wash and dry your cookgear and personal utensils daily.
4. Pack it in, pack it out.
5. Have a hygienic poo-poo plan.
6. Don't share too much.
7. Disinfect all water.

Cooking Tips and Other Bits of Friendly Advice

SPICE UP YOUR LIFE

The spice kit is the backcountry chef's best friend. We bring an extensive spice kit when using the Total Food Rationing plan, and even a limited one when we're carrying primarily pre-packaged foods.

The spice kit is the easiest way to make a good friend or a worst enemy. Remember to add spices a little bit at a time. Some spices, like the peppers, increase in strength as they cook, so wait a while between dashes. (A dash is less than a pinch. A pinch is about a 1/8 tsp.) It's relatively easy to go from cardboard flavor to red hot chili pepper-fire if you're not paying attention.

Use a spoon or a shaker-lid to add your spices to food. A whole canister of accidental curry is hard to choke down (even on potatoes). And your hands are dirty utensils. And take heed: rubbing your eye with cayenne is no fun.

If worse comes to worse, spices can be added to individual portions, which is especially useful if you have a companion who has had his "hot" buds surgically removed.

Don't carry your spices in film canisters. Yes, it's a handy size, but they're not safe for food unless you like eating plastic. Many small canisters are commercially available (Some are even sold with the spices in them!) or your can use baby bottle bags and tie a LOOSE knot in the top. Label your spices if you want.

Once they're individually packaged, carry all your spices together in a single bag: your spice kit.

POPULAR SPICES AND THEIR COMMON USES

SALT: White granules. Tastes like salt! Salt is added into almost all recipes but is not a required ingredient. If your food tastes bland or "soapy," it's probably because you need a little salt. Salt brings out the flavor. Remember: instant soups, bouillon, soy and tamari all contain salt, as do most pre-packaged meals. Salt is not a "bad" thing nutritionally, in fact, you need salt to function healthily. Too much salt is sometimes a problem for folks who have hypertension.

BAKING POWDER: Buy double-acting. This is a white powder that is used as a leavening agent in quick breads, cakes and biscuits.

BAKING YEAST: Light brown granules used in yeast bread recipes.

BASIL: Dark, green chopped leaves that smell sweet. Great in tomato and cream sauces. We use this a lot on pasta, pizzas, and potatoes.

BLACK PEPPER: Looks like ground up rock. We put this on almost every dish we make.

CAYENNE: Ground red pepper. Neon red powder that is very hot. Be careful.

CHILI PEPPER: Deep red granules. Spicy, used mostly in Mexican dishes.

CINNAMON: Fine brown powder with a strong sweet smell. Great in porridge, sweet breads, cobblers and cakes.

CRUSHED RED PEPPER: Red flakes with bits of yellow. Very hot. Use with caution.

CUMIN POWDER: Greenish-brown powder used in many Mexican dishes. Especially good on beans. This spice is commonly confused with curry powder.

CURRY POWDER: A gold powder with a strong smell and taste. Can be hot and spicy if you use enough. Food turns gold when you sprinkle it on. (At that point it's too late to turn back.) Used commonly in rice and fruit dishes.

DILL WEED: Looks like chopped thin grass. Smells like a sweet perfume. Good in creamy soups and sauces and breads.

GARLIC POWDER: Pale yellowish-white granules. Smells like garlic! Adds flavor to almost all of our dishes and keeps vampires away. $1/8$ tsp. equals about 1 clove of fresh garlic.

MRS. DASH: Comes commercial in a variety of mixes. Great on fish or any casserole to perk it up quickly. Lemon and garlic flavors are particular hits.

MUSTARD: Bright yellow powder. Tastes like a hot mustard. Good in cream sauces, pasta, and bean dishes.

ONION FLAKES: Hard white flakes that smell like onion. These need to be hydrated to be used for their best potential. 1 TBS. equals about $\frac{1}{2}$ a medium onion.

OREGANO: Light green leaf bits. Smells strong. Great in Italian dishes. Often mistaken for basil, but they interchange so nicely it really doesn't matter.

PARSLEY FLAKES: Greenish leafy bits. Good in pasta or grain dishes or sprinkled on fish.

CONDIMENTS

HOT SAUCES: These come in a variety of brands. Pick your favorite and bring a small plastic bottle along, especially on extended journeys.

SOY SAUCE OR TAMARI: Salty, dark liquid. Great in soups and sauces, over grains, and lentils. Good on popcorn. Can be purchased in a powdered form.

VANILLA EXTRACT: A brown liquid that smells sweet. Useful in baking and frostings. Nice addition to hot cereals and hot drinks.

VINEGAR: Clear or wine-colored, tangy liquid. We usually bring clear for its broader application. Useful in sweet and sour, salsas, and peanut butter sauces.

THICKENING AGENTS

Utilizing the crude measuring methods typically available in the backcountry, sometimes your soups, sauces, and even your main entrees end up too watery. Utilize any of the following ingredients to thicken your food: flour, potato flakes, an egg and milk powder mix, or even instant cereals. We like to mix them into a paste with water and then add them. It prevents, or at least limits, the chance of lumps. This works for tomato powder as well.

SPEEDING UP COOKING TIME

Choose a sheltered spot for the stove and use a wind shield, especially if it's windy. Heating the outdoors with a one-burner stove is a big project and you'll get hungry while you try. Many stoves are packaged with a wind shield or you can purchase them separately. Using the Pot Parka from Traveling Light also traps heat, and some pot sets are marketed with an optional heat exchanger. These can save a lot of time and fuel, especially on cold, high altitude trips.

Cooking with a lid cuts down on cooking time. Don't lift the lid or stir too often. This reduces the temperature and therefore the cooking time.

Pre-soaking dehydrated vegetables and beans throughout the day can save time. A water bottle works well for this. If you over-hydrate hash browns, they turn to mush.

To test for hydration, break a portion in half and look for dryness in the middle. If it's dry it's not hydrated. DO NOT pre-soak pasta!

PREVENTING BURNAGE!

If you are a beginner, the best way to prevent burning is to make sure you don't leave the kitchen while you're cooking. A watched pot will boil, despite claims otherwise … even claims in this book.

Make sure you use plenty of water. You can always add thickener later. Bring dishes to a boil, then reduce them to a simmer and stir occasionally. Add more water if you need it. Sticky is better than burnt.

Milk and cheese like to burn, so add them last and watch them carefully.

Margarine and oil burn less readily than butter. Margarine also spoils less readily than butter, so it's doubly good.

When you're frying it's OK to add a little water to help cook the ingredients and prevent burning. It cuts down on the crispy factor.

To prevent burning when baking, make sure your stove is on a low simmer and rotate the fry-bake pan frequently. To adjust the heat, hold your hand about 10 inches over the flame. You should be able to keep your hand there but still feel the heat. Keep as much heat as you want on the top of the pan while baking. Oil and flour the bottom of the fry-bake pan liberally. If you start to smell a strong, wonderful aroma— or burning—it's time to check.

PREVENTING ACCIDENTS

Keep everyone but the cook out of the kitchen. If it's too crowded, people kick things over and dinner ends up in the dirt. Even worse, boiling water ends up in someone's lap or boot.

If you have to cook under a tarp or tent vestibule, at least fill and light your stove somewhere far away. Nylon melts really quickly, even when it's raining. And ventilate the cook area well. Dying from carbon monoxide poisoning puts a damper on future trips.

Keep water handy. Twiggy fires gone wild and stoves kicked over can burn down the forest and you with it.

Don't pour hot water in hand held containers. Burns are one of the leading causes of backcountry evacuations.

Don't use your leg or any other part of your body as a cutting board. When using a knife cut away from yourself.

Fill your stove after every meal. If you have an emergency, your stove will always be ready.

TIPS FOR COLD WEATHER COOKING

Camp early. Cooking in the cold darkness lowers the fun factor. It also makes it harder to cook effectively.

Shelter is even more important in the cold. If there's deep snow on the ground, stamping or digging out a kitchen area (that can be filled in when you leave) not only makes a great, sheltered place to cook, but it warms you up at the same time.

Make a lot of hot drinks. They're a great source of calories and they make people happy.

Bring a light pair of gloves to wear while cooking. When it's "wicked" cold, merely touching your stove can cause frostbite. Avoid spilling fuel on flesh which can cause rapid cold injury.

Wipe the snow off the pots before placing them on the stove. The water dripping on the burner causes flame inconsistencies.

Cut your cheese, meats and margarine into chunks before leaving home. Even if they freeze solid, you can still break off some chunks . . . probably.

Put your munchables in the inside pocket of your parka. Food might thaw by snack time.

When melting snow for water, always keep some starter water. Snow melts faster in water. There is more surface area.

Go to bed with a quart of hot chocolate. It's fun to snuggle up to, and you can drink it in the night for a calorie boost.

Sleep with snacks. (Watch out in grizzly country.) Those 12 hour winter nights are a long time to go without eating.

Breakfasts

BUGG'S ALPINE START
(SERVES 1)

²/₃ cup potato flakes

2-3 Tbs. dry milk

1 glob of margarine

garlic powder, chili powder, salt and pepper to taste

²/₃-³/₄ cup of hot water

¹/₄ cup of cheese in small bits

HELPFUL HINTS: Heat water, milk, and butter. Stir in potatoes and cheese until just moist. Let stand for 30-60 seconds. Add spices and eat.

QUESADILLA A LA TAMAH
(SERVES 3-4)

1 dozen flour tortillas

1 lb. pepper jack cheese shredded at home

HELPFUL HINTS: Fiddle with your stove for ten minutes while swearing. Look for your stove cleaning kit and then realize you left it at home. Prime your stove and then realize there is only a little fuel left in it so you will have to start all over again. Heat your frying pan (over that stove you love so much). Put a tortilla in the pan, put some cheese on the tortilla. Wait for the cheese to melt. Fold the tortilla in half, pull it out of the pan, and eat it immediately while telling your partner that the next one is theirs.

STYLE POINTS: Add hydrated tomatoes or green pepper. Or salsa.

Thanks to Tamah V. Donaldson, Cal Adventures, Berkeley, CA.

BREAKFAST IN BED

1 cup quick oatmeal

4 Tbs. dry milk

small handful of raisins and nuts

$\frac{1}{2}$ Tbs. brown sugar

2 cups boiling water

HELPFUL HINTS: Make it in a thermos before bedding down. Snuggle up to the thermos in your sleeping bag and in the morning you have breakfast in bed. The cereal will stay relatively warm if you make it in a water bottle that has an insulated cover. Hey, it's better than getting up!

STYLE POINTS: Convince someone to bring you a cup of hot chocolate.

LEFTOVERS

Make too much dinner and refry it in the morning. Remember bacteria loves to grow on food, so this only works when it's really cold.

BAGELS

Bagels fried in butter and topped with cheese.

INSTANT SOUP

And the bread or biscuits you baked before going to bed. Grill the bread in your fry pan.

INSTANT BREAKFASTS

A powdered drink widely available at supermarkets. They don't fend off hunger and weakness very long, but they can give you a start. Try mixing them with hot water.

CEREAL: COLD

Cold cereal can be a nutritious, high fiber start to a backcountry day. We like to carry Grapenuts, Shredded Wheat, granola, and, sometimes, Raisin Bran. They can be mixed with fruit, dry milk, and water for a quick jumpstart in the morning.

HELPFUL HINTS: Mix the dry milk thoroughly into the cereal before adding the water. It prevents clumping. Mix two cereals together for variety. We like to eat our cold cereal hot. Just pour hot water on the top and eat away. Pick cereals that can be used in other ways such as baking. Grapenuts, for instance, make a great quick crust if you don't have graham crackers.

BARB'S GRANOLA: MAKE AT HOME

5 cups of oatmeal

1/2 cup raw cashews

1 cup of almonds

1 cup seame seeds

1 cup unsweetened coconut

1 cup wheat soy flour

1 cup non-instant powdered milk

1 cup wheat germ

1 cup raisins

1 cup honey

1 cup vegetable oil

Helpful Hints: Combine all dry ingredients. Mix honey and oil together. Blend dry with wet ingredients. Put on two baking trays. Bake at 325 degrees for 10 minutes. Cool and package.

Thanks to Barb Harper, Gunnison, CO and Lori Patin, Parlin, CO.

BACKCOUNTRY PAN-FRIED GRANOLA
(SERVES 3-4)

3 cups oatmeal

3-4 Tbs. margarine

1/2 cup brown sugar

1/2-1 cup nuts chopped into bits

1/2-1 cup raisins

HELPFUL HINTS: Melt margarine in fry pan. Add sugar and stir aggressively until it melts. Be careful: it likes to burn. (Try tipping the pan on edge and removing it from flame if sugar starts to burn.) Add all remaining ingredients and fry until brown.

STYLE POINTS: Add a couple of Tbs. of peanut butter and serve as a trail snack late in the trip after everyone has gobbled the gorp.

CEREAL: HOT

Although hot cereals have a bad name in many circles, they really can be a warm, tasty way to start the morning, and they are quick. Many people are turned off by their appearance and name. Stop calling them gruel, mush, and bloatmeal, and you'll have a lot easier time choking them down. You might even hear: "Please sir, I'd like some more."

PORRIDGE WITH A TWIST
(SERVES 2)

1 cups oats (non-instant)

2 cups water

$\frac{1}{4}$ cup dry milk

dash salt (optional)

$\frac{1}{4}$ cup raisins

$\frac{1}{4}$ cup dried chopped apples (or any fruit)

$\frac{1}{4}$ cup chopped nuts

$\frac{1}{2}$ tsp. cinnamon

sugar to taste

glob of margarine

HELPFUL HINTS: Bring oatmeal, dry milk, fruit, salt, and water to a boil. Simmer, stirring frequently, until porridge is the desired consistency. Top with margarine, sugar, cinnamon, and nuts. Takes about 10 minutes once water boils.

STYLE POINTS: We like to substitute $\frac{1}{4}$ cup oatmeal for $\frac{1}{4}$ cup Grapenuts or Shredded Wheat. It gives it a different texture.

POPULAR VARIATIONS ON THE THEME

CREAM OF WHEAT

Substitute 2 cups cream of wheat for oatmeal. Follow directions for Porridge With A Twist.

BREAKFAST COUSCOUS/ BULGUR/ RICE/GRITS

Substitute any of the preceding grains for oatmeal and follow the directions for Porridge With A Twist. Mixing different types together is always a hit. These take a little longer to cook.

CORN MEAL PUDDING

Substitute 1 cup of corn meal and 4 cups of water for the 1 cup of oatmeal and 2 cups of water in Porridge With A Twist. Proceed with the remaining directions.

INSTANT HOT CEREAL

Oatmeal, cream of wheat or rice, Malt O Meal, etc. Instant cereals usually require equal amounts of hot water and cereal. Boil water, add cereal, simmer one minute and set aside. Add desired amounts of sugar, fruit, nuts and spices.

EGGS FOR BREAKFAST

Fresh eggs will keep for a couple of weeks without refrigeration if they are not cracked. Backpacking without breaking them is almost impossible (unless you buy one of those plastic egg cases), but we've had some luck carrying them on paddling trips if they're carefully packed and used early. Most of the outdoor food companies package either powdered or freeze-dried egg breakfasts. We have tried most of these and find that they actually work. Because the portions are small, we prefer to combine them with things (potatoes, rice) rather than eat them separate. Egg powder can also be purchased bulk so you can add your own spices and choose your own portions. We carry egg powder but use it mostly for baking. Don't try to use freeze-dried eggs in baking. They don't work.

EGGS SCRAMBLED

$^1\!/_2$ cup egg powder

$^1\!/_4$ cup dry milk

1 cup water

spices

HELPFUL HINTS: Mix all ingredients thoroughly. Scramble in margarine. Add spices to taste.

MOM'S IMPOSSIBLE QUICHE

$^1\!/_2$ cup egg powder

$^1\!/_4$ cup dry milk

$^1\!/_2$ cup water

1-2 cups filling (hydrated veggies or meat)

1 cup sliced cheese

$^3\!/_4$ cup Essential Batter Mix (See Backcountry Baking) or
    commercial mix

spices to taste

HELPFUL HINTS: Mix together egg powder, dry milk, Basic Batter Mix and water. Spread filling in the bottom of fry-bake pan, cover with sliced cheese and add mixture. Stove-top bake for 20-30 minutes.

STYLE POINTS: Place the filling and the mixture on top of a pie crust (See Backcountry Baking).

Thanks to Elaine Dube, Kennebunk, ME.

POTATOES FOR BREAKFAST

ESSENTIAL HASH BROWNS
(SERVES 2-3)

2 cups dried hash browns

3 Tbs. margarine

1 cup sliced cheese

chili powder, garlic powder and pepper to taste

1⅓ cups of water

HELPFUL HINTS: Combine water, potatoes, and margarine in a non-stick skillet. Cook uncovered until all the water has been absorbed and bottom is brown. Flip with a spatula. Add spices and cheese. Cover until cheese has melted and the bottom is brown. Don't stir these. They will turn to mush and the bottom won't brown.

POPULAR VARIATIONS ON THE THEME

SCRAMBLED POTATOES AND EGGS
(SERVES 2-3)

2 cups dried hash browns

½ cup egg powder

¼ cup dry milk

2⅓ cups of water

3-4 Tbs. margarine

garlic, chili powder, black pepper to taste

1 cup of sliced cheese

HELPFUL HINTS: Follow Essential Hash Browns recipe. While browns are hydrating in fry pan, mix egg powder and dry milk with 1 cup water. As hydrated browns begin to fry, mix in eggs, add spices, and scramble. More margarine may be needed. Pull off heat, top with cheese and cover. When cheese is melted, serve.

STYLE POINTS: Carry one of the many scrambled egg or omelet mixes available through outdoor food companies. Substitute mix for egg mixture and spices. This works well with rice, too.

TRULY GOURMET

BROCK'S BEANS AND BROWNS
(SERVES 4)

2 cups dried hash browns and 4 cups hot water

1 cup instant refried beans and 1 cup hot water

1$\frac{1}{2}$ cups sliced cheese

$\frac{1}{4}$ cup egg powder/$\frac{1}{2}$ cup water/2 Tbs. dry milk/$\frac{1}{4}$ cup flour
   mixed

2 Tbs. margarine

garlic powder, chili powder, black pepper and cayenne to taste.

HELPFUL HINTS: Hydrate browns and beans separately. Mix egg/milk/ water/flour slurry into hydrated potatoes and pour them into the fry-bake pan atop the melted margarine. Position sliced cheese over the potatoes and top with beans/spice mixture. Stove-top bake 20 minutes or until done. Eggs must cook and cheese must melt. If you're in a rush, this recipe works well by merely rolling the crisped browns, cheese, and beans into a tortilla.

STYLE POINTS: Crisp the browns before baking. Serve with hot sauce, tortillas, sprouts, and sour cream.

Thanks to Mark Stivers, Lander, WY, and Kate Bartlett, Elaine Doll, Brett LeCompte, and Steve Mital of the Deer Hill School, Mancos, CO.

MARBLE MOUNTAIN MORNING CAKES
(MAKES 4-6 CAKES)

1 lb. dehydrated hash browns

$\frac{1}{4}$ lb. cheese

$\frac{1}{8}$ cup whole wheat flour

$\frac{1}{8}$ cup corn meal

raspberry jelly or preserves

HELPFUL HINTS: Cover potatoes with about 6-8 cups of boiling water. Set aside to hydrate (about 10 minutes). Be careful not to over-soak the potatoes or else they get soggy. Drain potatoes, saving a little water in the bottom. Add flour to mixture until you have a stiff batter. Form and flatten a cake in an oiled frying pan. Cook at medium-high heat, flipping when one side browns. After you flip, put a slice of cheese on the cake, add the lid onto the pan to melt the cheese. Serve topped with Raspberry Jelly Syrup.

Thanks to Michael Hock, Santa Fe, NM.

ESSENTIAL PANCAKES RECIPE
(SERVES 2-4)

2 cups Essential Batter Mix (See Backcountry Baking)

$1/4$ cup egg powder (optional)

1 Tbs. sugar (optional)

About $2^{1}/4$ cups of water

HELPFUL HINTS: Remember to adjust batter for the altitude (See Backcountry Baking). Slowly mix water into the dry ingredients until batter pours easily off spoon. If it's too thin, add more flour. Pour batter into bottom of a heated, oiled fry pan. Cook over medium heat until bubbles form on the top of the cake. Flip and cook until cake is golden brown and sounds hollow when tapped.

STYLE POINTS: Substitute buttermilk powder for milk powder in the Essential Batter Mix. Or add chopped nuts to the batter.

POPULAR VARIATIONS ON THE THEME

GRANOLA PANCAKES

$1^{1}/2$ cups Essential Batter Mix

$1/2$ cup granola

$1/4$ cup egg powder (optional)

About 2 cups of water

HELPFUL HINTS: Follow directions for Essential Pancakes.

APPLE PANCAKES

2 cups Essential Batter Mix (See Backcountry Baking)

1 package hot apple cider mix

1 package instant applesauce

$1/4$ cup egg powder (optional)

About $2^{1}/4$ cups water

HELPFUL HINTS: Follow the directions for Essential Pancakes.

STYLE POINTS: Add a $1/2$ cup of hydrated apple pieces to batter.

WILD AND HOTCAKES

2 cups Essential Batter Mix (See Backcountry Baking)

1 cup wild berries

2 Tbs. sugar

2-4 Tbs. egg powder (optional)

about 2 cups of water.

HELPFUL HINTS: Follow the directions for Essential Pancakes.

STYLE POINTS: Serve with Pick Your Own Syrup (from later in this chapter).

CORN GRIDDLE CAKES

$1^{1}/2$ cups cornmeal

$1/2$ cup whole wheat flour

2 tsp. baking powder

2 Tbs. oil

1 Tbs. sugar

$1/3$ cup dry milk

About 2 cups of water

HELPFUL HINTS: Slowly mix the water and oil into the dry ingredients. Cook as described in Essential Pancakes.

STYLE POINTS: Hydrate 1 cup of dried corn and add it to the batter before cooking.

BLOATMEAL PANCAKES

1 cup oatmeal

$1/3$ cup dry milk

2 Tbs. oil

$1/2$ cup flour

2 tsp. baking powder

1 Tbs. sugar (optional)

$1/4$ cup egg powder (optional)

About 2 cups of water

HELPFUL HINTS: Combine oatmeal, oil and water in pan and let it stand for 5-10 minutes to soften oats. Stir in the dry ingredients. Flip-bake as described under Essential Pancakes.

Style Points are rewarded to anyone who utilizes oatmeal in anything but a gruel.

CHOCOLATE LOVER'S PANCAKES

2 cups Essential Batter Mix (See Backcountry Baking)

$1/4$ cup egg powder (optional)

$1/4$ cup cocoa or $1/2$ cup hot chocolate mix

chocolate or carob chips

About $2 1/4$ cups water

HELPFUL HINTS: Follow the directions for Essential Pancakes.

TRULY GOURMET

HEALTH CAKES
(SERVES 3-4)

$^2/_3$ cup whole wheat

$^1/_3$ cup white flour

$^1/_4$ cup oatmeal or cornmeal

2 Tbs. wheat germ or bran

1 Tbs. sugar

2 tsp. baking powder

2 Tbs. egg powder

4 Tbs. buttermilk powder

1 Tbs. oil

About $1^1/_2$ cups of water

HELPFUL HINTS: Mix all dry ingredients. Slowly add oil and water. Cook as described in Essential Pancakes.

PANCAKE TOPPINGS

QUICK TOPPINGS

#1: brown sugar and margarine

#2: jelly

#3: instant applesauce

#4: peanut butter

CINNAMON BUTTER

$^1/_2$ cup sugar

$^1/_2$ tsp. cinnamon

$^1/_4$ cup. margarine

HONEY BUTTER

1/4 cup margarine
1/8 cup honey

BASIC SYRUP

1/2 cup sugar
1/4 cup water
1/4 cup margarine

HELPFUL HINTS: Simmer in small pan until sugar is dissolved and keep warm. Remember: sugar likes to burn.

STYLE POINTS: Add a tsp. of vanilla or a dash of cinnamon.

POPULAR VARIATIONS ON THE THEME

PICK YOUR OWN SYRUP

2 cups wild berries
1/2 cup sugar
water

HELPFUL HINTS: Pick the berry of your choice or any edible berry you can find. Simmer berries with sugar, smashing as you stir. Add water to desired consistency. Some berries require more sugar than others. For example, currants aren't very sweet while grouse whortleberries are very sweet. Add a little flour as thickener if you need it.

STYLE POINTS: Be able to distinguish good berries from bad berries.

HONEY SYRUP

1 cup honey
1 tsp. vanilla
2 Tbs. water
2 Tbs. margarine
1/2 cup coconut

HELPFUL HINTS: Heat all ingredients to desired consistency.

APPLE SYRUP

$^1/_2$ cup sugar

$^1/_2$ cup water

1 package hot apple cider mix

HELPFUL HINTS: Heat all ingredients to desired consistency.

JELLY SYRUP

$^1/_2$ cup of jelly

3 Tbs. margarine

HELPFUL HINTS: Heat ingredients to desired consistency.

TRULY SOMETHING

THE EYE-OPENER SYRUP

2 cups strong coffee

$^1/_2$ cup sugar

HELPFUL HINTS: Boil coffee continuously. Add sugar a spoonful at a time and stir. Boil until almost a syrup. It will thicken as it cools down. Pour over your pancakes for the best darn syrup you'll ever have outside of New England.

Thanks to David Tomco, Glastonbury, CT.

BREAKFAST BREADS

Don't put more than 2 -2$^1/_2$ cups of batter into a 9-10" fry-bake pan because it will raise up and stick to lid. Adjust recipes for altitude. (See Backcountry Baking)

SIN-A-MON BISCUITS

2 cups Essential Batter Mix or any commercially available mix

$^1/_2$ cup dry milk

$^1/_2$ cup oats (or leftover oatmeal)

$^{1}/_{2}$ cup brown sugar

2 tsp. cinnamon

1 handful of raisins

$^{3}/_{4}$ cup of water

HELPFUL HINTS: Combine dry ingredients and mix with wet. Fold gently until mixed. Bake in an oiled, heated, covered skillet until brown on one side. Flip and bake until brown.

Thanks to J. Scott McGee, Redmond, OR.

PSEUDOSCONES

$1^{1}/_{2}$ cups Essential Batter Mix (See Backcountry Baking)

$^{1}/_{2}$ cup flour

$^{1}/_{2}$ cup raisins

$^{1}/_{4}$ cup brown sugar

2 Tbs. egg powder (optional)

1 tsp. ground ginger

$^{1}/_{2}$ tsp. cinnamon

$^{1}/_{4}$ tsp. nutmeg

About $^{3}/_{4}$ cup of water

HELPFUL HINTS: Mix all ingredients into a stiff dough. Press into the bottom of a greased frypan. Cut dough with a spatula into 6-12 triangles. Stove-top bake.

STYLE POINTS: Serve with sugar/cinnamon or orange fruit crystals sprinkled on the top.

FRUITY FRITTERS

$1^{1}/_{2}$ cups Essential Batter Mix (See Backcountry Baking)

2 Tbs. egg powder (optional)

$^{3}/_{4}$ cup water

1 Tbs. sugar

1 cup dried chopped apples (or whatever)

$^{1}/_{2}$ tsp. cinnamon or nutmeg

HELPFUL HINTS: Hydrate apples. Combine all ingredients. Drop by spoonful into a hot fry pan. Fry in oil until crispy brown.

ESSENTIAL COFFEE CAKE
(SERVES 4)

2 cups Essential Batter Mix (See Backcountry Baking)

4-8 Tbs. sugar

2 Tbs. egg powder

$\frac{1}{2}$ tsp. salt

2 Tbs. oil or melted margarine

1 cup of water

HELPFUL HINTS: Mix all dry ingredient in a pan. Add the wet ingredients slowly until most of the lumps are gone. Scrape the batter into an oiled fry-bake pan. Cover the batter with one of the below toppings (or your own) and stove-top bake for 20-30 minutes.

STYLE POINTS: Add 1 package of sour cream mix to the dry ingredients and 1 tsp. of vanilla to the wet. Top with the Essential Coffee Cake Topping but use pecans as the nut.

TOPPING

$\frac{1}{2}$ cup brown sugar

1-2 tsp. cinnamon

2 Tbs. melted margarine

$\frac{1}{2}$ cup nuts (walnuts or almonds are good)

2 Tbs. flour or oatmeal (we prefer oatmeal)

HELPFUL HINTS: Mix all ingredients in a small pan or bowl and spread as best you can on top of the cake prior to baking it.

WILD MORNING COFFEE CAKE
(SERVES 4)

Follow Essential Coffee Cake recipe for batter.

STYLE POINTS: Substitute dry buttermilk for dry milk in Essential Batter Mix.

TOPPING

2 cups berries (anything non-poisonous will do)

1 cup dry milk

$1/4$-$1/3$ cup sugar (currants need a lot of sugar)

HELPFUL HINTS: Mix all ingredients together. Spoon on top of cake and stove-top bake.

TRULY GOURMET

MORNING STREUSEL

THE BATTER

$1^1/2$ cups of flour

2 tsp. baking powder

$1/4$ tsp. salt

$1/2$ cup of sugar

4 Tbs. margarine

2 Tbs. egg powder

2 Tbs. dry buttermilk or milk

$3/4$ cup water

HELPFUL HINTS: Combine all dry ingredients and then mix in the wet ones slowly. Pour half of mixture into an oiled fry-bake pan. Sprinkle with half of filling. Add other half of batter and filling. Stove-top bake for 20-30 minutes or until done.

THE FILLING

2 Tbs. flour

2 tsp. cinnamon

$1/2$ cup brown sugar

2 Tbs. melted margarine

$1/2$ cup chopped nuts

HELPFUL HINTS: Mix together in a bowl and set aside until needed.

YEAST CINNAMON SPIRAL

Make Essential Yeast Bread (See Backcountry Baking)

Fill with:

2 Tbs. flour

2 tsp. cinnamon

½ cup brown sugar

2 Tbs. melted margarine

½ cup chopped nuts

HELPFUL HINTS: Using your water bottle, roll dough into a thin rectangle on top of a plastic bag (more hygienic) or your foam-lite pad (less hygienic). Cover the rectangle with the filling, leaving about an inch around the edges. Roll dough into a tight tube and seal-pinch edges closed. If edges won't seal, dab a little water on them. Coil the dough into a spiral starting in the center of your fry-bake pan and working outward. If dough doesn't fill pan completely press it firmly into the bottom until it does. Stove-top bake until done. About 30 minutes.

If you're in a rush you can Flip-Bake (See Backcountry Baking), but the end product is denser.

STYLE POINTS: Cut rolled tube into 1-2 inch rounds and stove-top bake circles flat for cinnamon rolls (See Backcountry Baking).

Munchables

M unchables, or some people refer to them as lunchables, should total about 20% of your total food weight. Supermarkets, health food stores, and outdoor food companies provide a wide enough variety of these items to please almost any one. Below we've listed some of our favorites in terms of taste and durability.

BREADS AND CRACKERS

Bagels, tortillas, pita bread, pilot biscuits, melba toast, bagel chips, rye crisps, or any hardy cracker.

TRAIL MIXES

Trail mixes are widely available in a variety of mixtures. Over the years we've phased them out of our diet in favor of carrying items individually and then mixing them in small amounts. Why? We spent too many dim-lit evenings picking things out of the mixes to use in baking, like the chocolate chips, and we grew tired of traveling companions "mining" the M&Ms out of the gorp. Buy trail mixes if you're in a rush, or build your own if you're picky about the contents.

MEAT, PEANUT BUTTER, AND CHEESE

These items are usually represented in the 13% of your total food weight entitled High Calorie. They make great munchables, especially on cool weather trips. The harder cheeses (Cheddar, Swiss, Colby, Edam, Gouda) last longer without spoiling. If you leave the cheese vacuum-packed until you're ready to eat, it won't mold. Many summer sausages and pepperoni need no refrigeration until the casing is broken. Buy them in small packages and plan to share them at one lunch or dinner. Peanut butter is high calorie but has no cholesterol. It's not as versatile as meat or cheese, but it's good for variety. Peanut butter is also good in soups, sauces, and breads.

DRIED FRUITS AND NUTS

Carry them separately or toss them into trail mixes. They are high calorie for their weight.

FRESH FRUITS AND VEGETABLES

Hardy fruits and vegetables make great snacks, but they're not light. We often carry apples and carrots.

CANDY AND GRANOLA BARS

Remember chocolate melts in the heat. Hard candies are occasionally nice to have in your pocket, especially for energy snacks on the go.

COOKIES

We usually carry fruit bars. They're high calorie but low fat, and if you crush them it doesn't matter . . . they just clump together. Whatever you like, try to pick cookies that won't immediately turn to dust if you stuff your sleeping bag onto them. If you discover dust, use it to make a no-bake pie or dump the crumbs into a pudding.

JERKY

Although it's hard to find, salmon jerky is our favorite. Jerky can also be hydrated and added to meals.

ENERGY BARS AND DRINKS

We carry them. They're low fat and a nice boost for that last couple of miles to camp.

MUNCHABLES TO MAKE IN THE BACKCOUNTRY

It doesn't seem to matter how many munchables you bring with you, they will be gone before the end of your trip. Don't berate your companions for eating more than their share of the trail mix. Impress them with your ability to take the bits and pieces of the remaining stores and turn them into tasty treats.

SCOOBY-SNACKS

Follow the Essential Pan Biscuits recipe (See Backcountry Baking). Sweeten the biscuits with sugar and raisins or add some nuts. Leftover crumbs of cookies or graham crackers combine nicely. Top them with cheese, peanut butter, margarine, or eat them alone.

Thanks to Dan Robison, Block Island, RI.

INSTANT SOUPS AND INSTANT POTATOES

A quick lunch if you can spare the time to boil water. Ramen noodles only take 3 minutes once the water has boiled. This is an especially nice break on a cold, windy day.

PAN FRY GRANOLA (See Breakfast), PAN BISCUITS, SWEET BREADS, and CAKES (See Backcountry Baking) can become lunch.

MUNCHABLES TO MAKE AT HOME

After cooking any of the bars described below, cool them thoroughly in the refrigerator, then cut them and freeze them until use. If you don't cool and freeze them, they tend to break apart and get eaten at home!

SOLO BAR

6 eggs

1 lb. brown sugar

1 lb. white sugar

1/2 tsp. vanilla extract

4 tsp. baking soda

1/2 lb. butter

1 1/2 lbs. crunchy peanut butter

9 cups oatmeal

1 lb. chocolate chips

1/2 lb. raisins

sunflower seeds

1 cup shredded coconut (keeps the bars moist)

HELPFUL HINTS: Mix in order given. Bake on two jelly roll sheets at 350 degrees until done. Sides will pull away and become golden brown. Don't over cook or they become hard and crispy instead of thick and chewy.

Thanks to Ruthe Hubbell, Conway, NH.

FRUIT BARS

1 cup chopped walnuts
½ cup raisins
½ cup dried apricots
⅓ cup orange juice
1½ cups flour
½ tsp. baking powder
½ tsp. salt
½ tsp. cinnamon
½ cup butter
½ brown sugar
2 eggs
1 cup diced candied fruit

GLAZE
1 cup powdered sugar
1 Tbs. hot water
1½ tsp. melted butter
¼ finely diced candied fruit

HELPFUL HINTS: Cut apricots into small pieces and combine with raisins and orange juice. Sift together flour, baking powder, salt and cinnamon and set aside. Cream together butter, sugar, and brown sugar. Beat in 2 eggs. Stir in fruit mixture and flour mixture. Stir in walnuts and candied fruit. Spread in a 9" x 13" pan and bake at 375 degrees until done. Cool and spread with Glaze.

DEEP IN THE CONGO BARS

2¾ cups of flour
2½ tsp. baking powder
½ tsp. salt
⅔ cup shortening or butter
1 lb. dark brown sugar

3 eggs

1 cup chopped walnuts or pecans

½ lb. chocolate chips

HELPFUL HINTS: Mix baking powder, flour and salt. Melt shortening and add brown sugar. Allow it to cool slightly and add eggs. Beat well. Add dry ingredients. Stir in chips and nuts. Bake at 350 degrees for 25-30 minutes.

SEVEN SUMMITS BAR

½ stick butter

1 cup graham cracker crumbs

1 cup shredded coconut

2 cups mixed chocolate and butterscotch chips

1 can sweet condensed milk

¾ cup oatmeal

1 cup chopped walnuts

HELPFUL HINTS: Layer in a 9" x 13" pan in the order listed and bake at 350 degrees for 20 minutes. Cool thoroughly, cut into bars and freeze until ready to use.

SPLIT LEVEL RUINS
(RUINS YOUR APPETITE)

1 cup chocolate chips

3 oz. cream cheese

⅓ cup evaporated milk

½ cup chopped walnuts

2 Tbs. seame seeds

½ tsp. almond extract

1½ cups flour

½ tsp. baking powder

¼ tsp. salt

¾ cup sugar

½ cup soft margarine

1 egg

½ cup oatmeal

HELPFUL HINTS: Melt together chocolate, cream cheese and milk over low heat. Stir constantly. Remove from heat and stir in walnuts, seeds, and almond extract. Combine remaining ingredients and press them into the bottom of an oiled baking pan (8" x 11"). Pour chocolate mixture on the top and spread evenly. Sprinkle with oatmeal. Bake at 375 degrees until done. About 20 minutes. Cool.

QUEST BREAD

4 cups whole wheat flour

⅓ cup wheat germ

¾ cup brown sugar

⅓ cup oil

¼ cup molasses

4 Tbs. dry milk

1½ tsp salt

1½ tsp. baking powder

¼ cup sunflower seeds

1 cup water

HELPFUL HINTS: Combine all ingredients and mix thoroughly. Bake in an oiled 8" x 8" pan at 300 degrees for approximately 1 hour. Cool, cut into squares and put in a plastic bag. Make sure bread is cool and dry when you package it. This bread will last for weeks without growing mold.

NUTTY TREATS

Nuts are high in calories and a great source of protein. Unfortunately, they are also a great source of fat. But it's mostly monounsaturated fat (except in coconut, that's why it's so moist and tasty), and they have no cholesterol. Mix nuts into snacks for a nutritional boost.

GOOP BALLS
(OR JUST GOOP)

About 1 cup peanut butter

$^1\!/_2$ cup granola

$^1\!/_2$ cup dry milk

$^1\!/_4$ cup brown sugar

$^1\!/_4$ cup raisins

$^1\!/_2$ cup of chopped nuts

HELPFUL HINTS: Mix granola, milk, sugar, raisins and nuts in a bowl or pan. Add enough peanut butter to make the mixture stiff but not crumbly. Roll into golf balls and store chilled. You can also mix this in a plastic bag and eat it by the spoonful for lunch.

STYLE POINTS: Roll balls in coconut before serving. Add chocolate chips instead of nuts.

SPICED NUTS

2 cups dry-roasted, unsalted nuts

1-2 Tbs. hot sesame oil

1-2 Tbs. garlic tamari (or soy sauce and 1/8 tsp. garlic powder)

$^1\!/_2$ tsp. cayenne

HELPFUL HINTS: Mix all ingredients together in a bowl. Spread them on a baking sheet and bake at 350 degrees for 30 minutes. Stir them 2 or 3 times while baking. Allow nuts to cool and then package them in a plastic container.

NUBBLES
(NUTS AND NIBBLES)

4-5 cups of dry cereal (Crispex, Fruit Wheats, Rice/Wheat/Corn Chex, etc.)

1 cup unsalted pretzels broken into bits

2 cups unsalted dry-roasted nuts

$^1\!/_3$ cup margarine

$1^1\!/_2$ Tbs. Worcestershire sauce

1 tsp. onion powder

½-1 tsp. garlic powder

1 tsp. celery flakes

HELPFUL HINTS: Heat margarine, Worcestershire, and spices. Add to cereal mixture and mix. Add nuts and stir. Bake at 300 degrees on a baking sheet for 10 minutes.

STYLE POINTS: OK, add chocolate bits after the mixture cools.

MA'S SUGARY PEANUTS

4 cups raw, shelled peanuts

2 cups sugar

1 cup water

HELPFUL HINTS: Mix sugar and water in a large frypan. Add peanuts and bring to a boil. Simmer for 15-20 minutes. Stir constantly the last few minutes until the liquid crystallizes on the nuts. Spread on a baking sheet and bake at 325 degrees for 15 minutes.

STYLE POINTS: Add a tsp. of flavoring: vanilla, chocolate, etc.

Thanks to Eris Mozingo Tilton, Putney, GA.

Sauces

Grains, pasta, and potatoes are just carbohydrates without sauce. And although we know carbohydrates power us around the backcountry, it's the sauces that make them tasty meals. Here's a few to get started. Remember the fun is making them your own by changing the nonessential ingredients.

BASIC CREAM SAUCE
MAKES ABOUT ONE CUP

	Thin	Medium	Thick
Milk (4 Tbs. dry & 1 cup water)	1 cup	1 cup	1 cup
Flour	1 Tbs.	2 Tbs.	3 Tbs.
Margarine	1 Tbs.	2 Tbs.	3 Tbs.

HELPFUL HINTS: As you can see above, you can vary the measurements quite a bit and still get cream sauce, so don't worry about it too much if you don't have a measuring device. Melt margarine in bottom of pan over low heat, add flour stirring constantly, to prevent burning, until mixture is as smooth as possible. Add reconstituted milk, slowly stirring constantly to prevent burning. Keep stirring over low heat until it is thick enough. This usually takes about 5 minutes. Take it off the heat and add salt and pepper to taste.

POPULAR VARIATIONS ON THE THEME

CHEESE SAUCE

1 cup Basic Cream Sauce
1/2 to 1 cup of your favorite cheese

HELPFUL HINTS: Make the Basic Cream Sauce first, cut the cheese into small bits and add it at the end with the pot off the burner. Remember: cheese loves to burn.

MUSTARD CHEESE SAUCE

1 cup Basic Cream Sauce

$1/2$ cup cheese

$1/4$ tsp. garlic powder

$1/4$ tsp. mustard powder (or a Tbs. of mustard)

dash of cayenne or Tabasco

ALFREDO

1 cup Basic Cream Sauce

$1/2$ cup parmesan cheese

$1/2$ tsp. basil or dill

$1/4$ tsp. garlic

salt and pepper to taste

BROWN GRAVY

1 cup Basic Cream Sauce

1 tsp. onion flakes

$1/4$ tsp. garlic powder

1-2 Tbs. soy sauce or tamari

HELPFUL HINTS: Add a beef or chicken bouillon cube instead of the soy for a "meat" option. Don't do both or it will be too salty. These sauces are great on pan biscuits for breakfast.

TOMATO CREAM SAUCE

1 cup Basic Cream Sauce

2 Tbs. tomato base

$^{1}/_{2}$ tsp. garlic powder

1 tsp. basil

HELPFUL HINTS: Use 2 cups of instant tomato soup instead of base and spices. Serve on pasta.

ASIAN TOMATO SAUCE

1 cup Basic Cream Sauce

2 Tbs. tomato base

$^{1}/_{4}$ teaspoon of ground ginger

1 Tbs. onion flakes

soy sauce or tamari to your liking

HELPFUL HINTS: Serve on bulgur or rice.

PEANUT BUTTER SAUCES

PEANUT BUTTER GRAVY
(MAKES ABOUT 1$^{1}/_{2}$ CUPS)

$^{1}/_{2}$ cup peanut butter (crunchy is better)

$^{1}/_{4}$ tsp. garlic powder

2 Tbs. vinegar (optional)

3 Tbs. dry milk (optional)

1 cup hot water

1$^{1}/_{2}$ Tbs. soy sauce

cayenne

HELPFUL HINTS: Heat water, remove from burner and add other ingredients. Reheat carefully if need arises. Peanut butter loves to scorch your pan. Excellent on spaghetti noodles.

HOT SESAME-PEANUT SAUCE

$\frac{1}{2}$ cup peanut butter (crunchy is better)

1 cup hot water

2 Tbs. vinegar (optional)

3 tsp. hot sesame oil

$1\frac{1}{2}$ soy sauce or tamari

1 tsp. onion flakes

$\frac{1}{2}$ tsp. crushed hot red pepper

HELPFUL HINTS: Heat water, remove from burner and add other ingredients.
Excellent served hot or cold over noodles.

CURRY SAUCE

1 Tbs. of oil

1 Tbs. flour

2 tsp. onion flakes

1 cup water

$\frac{1}{4}$ cup dried chopped apples

$\frac{1}{4}$ cup raisins

1 tsp. brown sugar

$1\frac{1}{2}$-2 tsp. curry powder

$\frac{1}{2}$ tsp. salt

HELPFUL HINTS: Heat oil and flour stirring constantly over low heat until the mixture
is smooth. Add spices, water and fruit. Bring to a boil and simmer until apples are tender. Serve over lentils, rice, bulgur, or couscous.

ITALIAN TOMATO SAUCE

½ cup tomato powder

1 Tbs. onion flakes

½ Tbs. parsley

½ tsp. basil or oregano

½ Tbs. oil

¼ tsp. garlic powder

1½-2 cups of water (more for thinner sauce)

Optional: Dried tomatoes, mushrooms, peppers, etc.

HELPFUL HINTS: Bring water and any dehydrated vegetables you are using to a boil. Add the rest of the ingredients and simmer, stirring frequently over low heat until you are satisfied with the flavoring and consistency. Great sauce for pasta, lasagna, and pizza.

MEXICAN SAUCE

2-3 Tbs. tomato powder

1 cup of hot water (more for thinner sauce)

1 Tbs. onion flakes

½ - 1 tsp. chili powder

½ tsp. cumin

½ basil or oregano

¼ tsp. garlic powder

1 Tbs. oil

1 Tbs. corn meal or flour

black pepper

2 Tbs. red and green peppers (optional)

Dried tomatoes (optional)

HELPFUL HINTS: Rehydrate vegetables in hot water. Heat oil, seasonings, and corn meal in bottom of pan. Combine all ingredients and simmer, stirring frequently for 5-10 minutes. Great on beans, rice, bulgur or pizza.

Soups

S oups are a great pick-me-up before meals and a wonderful lunch on a cold day with breads or snacks. You can make soups quickly with the ingredients you carry in your pack, or there are lots of quick soups available at your local store or outdoor shop. We tend to stock up on instant soups at the grocery store. They are quick, inexpensive (though salty), and make great flavorings when added to grains and potatoes. Soups are also a great way to get rid of left-overs or to use up bits and pieces of food at the end of a trip.

ESSENTIAL BROTH SOUP

6 cups water

2-3 bouillon cubes or 2-3 pkg. instant soup

1/4 cup margarine

1-2 cups filler: grains, pasta, potatoes, vegetable, cheese, etc.

spices

HELPFUL HINTS: Boil the water and add bouillon. Be careful, this is salty. Add solid ingredients and spices. Simmer until done.

POPULAR MIXES

MISO SOUP: Cup of miso soup, dried tofu, noodles, onion flakes, garlic powder, and black pepper.

CHICKEN SOUP: Chicken bouillon, dried vegetables, noodles or rice, and curry powder.

TOMATO BEEF: Tomato Powder and beef or vegetable bouillon, dried vegetables, noodles, black pepper, basil, and garlic powder.

LENTIL SOUP: Lentils, tomato base, vegetable bouillon, onion flakes, garlic powder, cumin, chili powder and black pepper.

TRULY GOURMET

DUMPLINGS

1 cup Essential Batter Mix (See Backcountry Baking)
about $^1/_3$ cup water

HELPFUL HINTS: Mix dry and wet ingredients. Drop batter by spoonful onto the top of the bubbling soup. Simmer uncovered until the dumplings are done. About 10 minutes.

STYLE POINTS: Add herbs or cheese to your dumpling batter.

ESSENTIAL CREAMY SOUP

6 cups water
2-3 bouillon cubes or 2-3 pkg. instant soup
$^1/_4$ cup margarine
1-2 cups filler: grains, pasta, potatoes, vegetable, cheese, etc.
$^1/_2$-1 dry milk
$^1/_4$ flour or potato flakes, buds or pearls (thickener)
spices

HELPFUL HINTS: Bring water to boil then add bouillon, spices and fillers. Simmer until fillers are tender. Mix thickener into a paste with a small bit of water. Slowly add the paste to the soup stirring constantly until thick. Add milk and any cheese last.

POPULAR MIXES

TOMATO: Tomato base, rice, black pepper, oregano, garlic powder, milk and thickener.

CHOWDER: Vegetable bouillon, dried corn and potatoes, black pepper, basil, garlic, milk, and thickener.

CREAM OF BROCCOLI: 2 pkgs. instant cream of broccoli soup, dried potatoes, and black pepper.

CREAM OF CHICKEN: 2 pkg. instant creamy chicken vegetable soup, rice, black pepper, and thickener.

Entrees

GRAINS, GRAINS, GRAINS

A native grain of Asia, rice is the staple food for over half the folks in the world. There are many different types of rice sold in the U.S. In terms of shapes, long-grain rice grains are approximately 4 times longer than they are wide and cook up real fluffy; medium-grain rices are softer and tend to cook up more tender; and short-grain rice is the stickiest.

Brown rice is the whole unpolished rice grain with only the husk and a bit of bran removed. White rice has been husked and polished, with bran and germ removed. Brown rice takes about twice as long to cook as white rice and has a nuttier, chewier flavor. Precooked or instant rice is the most expensive, the most processed, and the least nourishing. We usually cook with instant rice only in situations where we need to save fuel. Brown and white rice are now available at the local supermarket in instant and non-instant forms.

Wild rice, amazingly enough, is not really rice but the seed of a water grass native to the Northern Great Lakes. It's very nutritious and a great way to add style points to any meal, in addition to being very expensive.

Bulgur is the "rice" of the Middle East. It is really not rice either but cracked wheat that has been parboiled (steamed and dried) and cracked into small bits. You see it more commonly at supermarkets these days, but it can be readily found in bulk at health food stores and co-ops. Bulgur has a nutty flavor. It is great mixed with rice or in any recipe that calls for rice. It cooks faster than rice. People that call bulgur vulgar have not been introduced to it correctly.

Couscous is the bulgur of North Africa. It's finely cracked wheat or millet that has been parboiled and refined. It cooks very quickly.

Other grains that are available for a change of pace include: millet (takes a lot of time and water to cook), barley (available in quick cooking form), kasha or buckwheat groats (an Eastern European grain with a nut-like flavor), and corn grits (which can be hard to get outside of the South).

These days, there are many companies from which to buy pre-packaged grain mixtures of different flavors right at the supermarket. Several companies market meals prepared specifically for outdoor travelers. Many of these options are tasty, but they tend to be expensive, and depending on the brand you pick, can have many additives, especially salt. Unless we are traveling where time and ease of cooking are more of an issue than money and flavor, we prefer to cook our grain dishes from scratch. We often will throw a commercial mix or two in the foodbag for a change of pace or at the end of a long day. If you buy commercial mixes make sure you are at least getting a 1½ serving per person. Ready-made mixes tend to overestimate the number of people they will serve.

ESSENTIAL GRAIN RECIPE
(YIELDS ABOUT 2½-3 CUPS/SERVES 2)

1 cup grain

2 cups water (for wild rice, millet, barley add 3 cups)

HELPFUL HINTS: Wait for the water to boil to add the grain. (It's not required, but it makes the grain less sticky.) Simmer with pot covered so water does not evaporate before the grain is soft. Do not stir grain unless you like it sticky and clumped together. To prevent burning, as the water is absorbed tip the pot to the side periodically to assure there is a small amount of water in the bottom. If the water is gone and the grain is still crunchy, it is acceptable to add more water, preferably hot, but it's not required. Bulgur, Couscous, and Kasha take about 15-20 minutes. White rice will cook about twice as fast as brown rice (30 minutes vs. 1 hour). If you prefer brown rice or barley, we suggest buying quick-cooking style, especially if you are traveling above 10,000 feet. It can take a lot of fuel at higher elevations.

SERVING SUGGESTIONS: A quick way to make basic grains more interesting is to cook them with one or two instant soups. Cream of chicken, creamy tomato, and cream of mushroom are consistent favorites. Serve with a Curry or Mexican Sauce (See Sauces). Cook grains and then fry them with nuts, herbs and spices and a bit of leftover pasta. Cook grains, add cream sauce, top with nuts, cheese, and bread crumbs and bake. Mixing grains together is a treat as well, but remember some take longer to cook than others. Dried vegetables improve the appearance and sometimes the flavor of your grain dishes.

POPULAR VARIATIONS ON THE THEME

CREAMY NUT PILAF
(SERVES 2-3)

1 cup rice or bulgur

2 cups water

1 bouillon cube

1 cup Basic Cream Sauce (See Sauces)

$^{1}/_{3}$ cup parmesan cheese

$^{1}/_{3}$ cup sunflower seeds

salt and pepper to taste

HELPFUL HINTS: Cook rice with bouillon cube and water. Set aside. Prepare Basic Cream Sauce, adding cheese and seeds last.

STYLE POINTS: Include a $^{1}/_{3}$ cup of orzo pasta and $^{1}/_{2}$ cup dried mushrooms to the original cooking.

SPANISH RICE
(SERVES 2-4)

1 cup rice

2 cups water

1 bouillon cube

1 Tbs. oil

$^{1}/_{3}$ cup dried red and green pepper

1 cup dried tomatoes

2 cups instant tomato soup

1-2 Tbs. onion flakes

$^{1}/_{2}$ tsp. garlic powder

$^{1}/_{2}$ tsp. basil

$^{1}/_{2}$ tsp. oregano

$1/2$ tsp. chili powder

$1/2$-1 cup grated cheddar

black pepper and cayenne to taste

HELPFUL HINT: Cook rice, water, onion flakes, dried peppers, tomatoes, and instant soup. Place oil in frying pan. Add rice mixture and spices. Fry to desired crispiness, top with cheese,cover, and set aside to allow cheese to melt.

STYLE POINTS: Great with bulgur instead of rice. Use fresh onions and garlic. Serve with tortillas and sour cream dip.

QUICK CURRIED RICE
(SERVES 3-4)

1 cup rice

1 Tbs. onion flakes

1 tsp. curry powder

1 vegetable bouillon cube

2 Tbs. dried red and green peppers

3 cups water

1 cup dried apples, raisins, apricots cut into small bits

$1/2$ cup cashews and/or peanuts

$1/3$ cup coconut (optional)

HELPFUL HINTS: Bring water, rice, bouillon cube to a boil. Simmer. When water is half absorbed add fruit, peppers, and spices. Simmer until done. Mix in nuts, cover with coconut and serve.

STYLE POINTS: Use couscous instead of rice. When couscous, fruit and spices are done, fry in oil with nuts. Sprinkle with coconut and serve with chapatis.

FRIED RICE
(SERVES 2-3)

1 cup rice

2 cups water

2 Tbs. onion flakes

2 Tbs. dried red and green peppers

2 Tbs. soy sauce

$^1/_4$ tsp. garlic powder

1 Tbs. oil

a mixture of 4 Tbs. egg powder, 1 Tbs. dry milk, and $^1/_2$ cup water

black pepper to taste

sunflower seeds

HELPFUL HINTS: Cook rice with onion flakes and any vegetables you include. Put oil in frying pan and scramble reconstituted eggs. Add all ingredients and fry until they are thoroughly hot.

STYLE POINTS: Cook one package of ramen noodles and fry them with rice. Use garlic tamari instead of soy sauce. Add $^1/_2$ cup dried mushrooms and/or $^1/_2$ cup dried peas and carrots. Top with cashews.

MEXICAN RICE CASSEROLE
(SERVES 3-4)

1 cup rice or grits

1 cup freeze-dried corn

1-2 Tbs. onion flakes

1-2 cups cheddar cut into small bits

$^1/_3$ cup dry milk

$^1/_2$ tsp. each chili pepper, salt and pepper

about 3 cups water

HELPFUL HINTS: Cook rice, water, corn, milk and spices. Mix all ingredients. Pour into fry-bake pan. Cover and warm over low heat until cheese melts.

STYLE POINTS: Serve with tortillas and sour cream dip. Salsa or hot sauce makes a nice addition as well.

QUICK SWEET AND SOUR RICE
(SERVES 3-4)

1/4 cup red and green peppers

1/4 cup raisins or apricots

1/4 cup pineapple chunks

3 Tbs. soy sauce

1 cup rice

3 cups water

3 oz. dried tofu or chicken (optional)

1 pkg. of sweet and sour mix

HELPFUL HINTS: Pour about a cup of hot water over dried tofu/meat, fruit and peppers. Cook rice with 2 cups water. Add sweet and sour mix to fruit and vegetable mix. Return to a boil. Pour over rice. Mix and serve.

STYLE POINTS: Serve with almonds.

RICE AND POTATO PATTIES

1 cup cooked rice

4 Tbs. dry milk

2/3 cup instant potato

1/2 cup cheese cut into small bits

Garlic powder, salt and pepper to taste

2 Tbs. margarine

HELPFUL HINTS: Boil water, milk and margarine. Remove from heat, add cheese, instant potato, rice and set aside for a couple of minutes. Spice to taste, form into patties and fry in margarine or oil. (Great use for leftover rice. If you cooked it with a couple of instant soups it's even better.)

STYLE POINTS: Cover with Brown Gravy. Add a few sunflower seeds.

TRULY GOURMET

CHICKEN CURRY
(SERVES 4)

2 oz. freeze-dried chicken

1 package freeze-dried peas

1 env. Knorr Leek Soup

1 env. Herb-Ox Instant Chicken Broth

3-4 tsp. curry powder

1½ cups instant rice

Coconut flakes/cashews/raisins or dried cranberries

HELPFUL HINTS: Bring 5-6 cups of water to a boil. Add chicken, peas, leek soup mix and chicken broth. Set aside to rehydrate (15-30 minutes). Add curry powder. Bring back to a boil and add minute rice. Cook 5-10 minutes until tender, stirring occasionally. Sprinkle with coconut, cashews, and raisins and serve.

Thanks to Iretta Hunter, Danville, CA.

PASTA

Most outdoor folks we know are addicted to pasta. It's quick, filling, readily available in wonderfully different shapes and colors, and can even be tasty if you cook it right. We've climbed several high peaks on pasta alone so you can trust us on this: mac and cheese gets old 14 days straight. You can buy pasta in ready-made dishes. We find they are usually too small and expensive for common outdoor use.

ESSENTIAL PASTA RECIPE
(SERVES APPROXIMATELY 3-4)

3 cups pasta

6 cups water

1 tsp. oil (optional)

OR 1 part pasta to 2 parts water

HELPFUL HINTS: Heat water to a rolling boil, add oil, and pasta. Cook pasta until it is tender. The time can vary a lot. Angel hair and Chinese noodles take a short time (3-5 minutes) versus shells and whole wheat elbows which take longer (12-15 minutes). Fettuccini and spaghetti are somewhere in the middle. Altitude will add to the cooking time since the water is boiling at a lower temperature. Choose your pastas carefully if you will be traveling above 10,000 feet. Whole wheat and vegetable pastas require the longest cooking times and often go from still crunchy to glue without ever reaching that "perfect " moment. IMPORTANT: If you add the pasta before the water boils you are guaranteed to be left with wall paper paste instead of dinner. Pasta loves company . . . in other words, test pasta frequently to avoid mushy problems.

SERVING SUGGESTIONS: Any of the cream sauces or peanut butter sauces combine with pasta well. (See Sauces for recipes.)

SERVING SIZE: A pound of pasta generally satisfies 4 folks if you're also having soup and bread or dessert. We do know many hardy hikers who can easily consume 8 ounces themselves. On cold long days of hiking we (the authors) regularly split a pound of pasta. But on warm desert nights we get by splitting a half a pound. So, what's the answer? Play around until you figure it out.

POPULAR VARIATIONS ON THE THEME

FETTUCCINI ALFREDO
(SERVES 3-4)

1 lb. of fettuccini

1^1/$_2$-2 cups of Alfredo Sauce (See Sauces)

parmesan cheese

HELPFUL HINTS: Make the Alfredo Sauce first and set aside. Cook and drain pasta. Warm sauce, stirring constantly. Add to pasta and serve.

STYLE POINTS: Add hydrated vegetables for a primavera touch or seafood you harvested yourself.

ITALIAN SPAGHETTI
(SERVES 3-4)

1 lb. thin spaghetti noodles

1½ - 2 cups Italian Tomato Sauce (See Sauces)

parmesan cheese

HELPFUL HINTS: Prepare Italian Tomato Sauce. Cook and drain pasta. Warm sauce, add to pasta, and serve with parmesan cheese.

STYLE POINTS: Add lentils, falafel balls, summer sausage or hydrated beef to your sauce. It's also a good protein boost.

MACARONI AND CHEESE
(SERVES 3-4)

3 cups of elbows or shells

1½ -2 cups Mustard Cheese Sauce (See Sauces)

¼ cup sunflower seeds

2 Tbs. onion flakes

HELPFUL HINTS: Prepare the Mustard Cheese Sauce first, adding the onion flakes with the other sauce ingredients. Cook and drain pasta. Add warmed sauce, add seeds and serve.

For Quick Mac and Cheese leave about a cup of water when draining the noodles, add all ingredients for sauce to the pot and warm slowly over a low flame.

STYLE POINTS: Add hydrated peas and tuna for a Tuna Casserole Deluxe. Serve with croutons.

ALPINE SPAGHETTI
(SERVES 3-4)

1 lb. thin spaghetti

4 Tbs. oil

1 cup parmesan cheese

4-6 tsp. ground sweet basil

1-2 Tbs. parsley flakes

garlic powder and pepper to taste

HELPFUL HINTS: Cook and drain pasta. Add oil and toss, then mix in the remaining ingredients.

Thanks to Kitty Ann and Roger Cox, Pitkin, CO.

AMERICAN CHOP SUEY
(SERVES 3-4)

3 cups of elbows or shells

2 cups cream of tomato instant soup (2 packets) or 2 cups
    Tomato Cream Sauce (See Sauces)

1-2 Tbs. onion flakes

1/4 cup dried red and green peppers (optional)

1 cup dried ground beef or any type of hardy sausage cut into
    small bits

HELPFUL HINTS: Cook and drain pasta. Add dried ground beef, onion flakes and dried peppers to 2 cups of water, bring to a boil, simmer 5-10 minutes to hydrate the ingredients. Add tomato soups, mix all ingredients, and serve with black pepper.

HOT RED PEPPER PASTA
(SERVES 2-4)

1 lb. linguine or fettuccini

1/4 cup olive oil

2 tsp. minced garlic or garlic powder to taste

1 tsp. crushed red pepper

2 Tbs. parsley flakes

HELPFUL HINTS: Cook and drain pasta. Heat oil and sauté garlic. (Skip this step if using garlic powder.) Add remaining ingredients and toss until pasta is coated. Be careful with the crushed red pepper.

STYLE POINTS: Top with parmesan and tamari to taste.

SPAGHETTI A LA CARBONDALE
(SERVES 3-4)

1 lb. thin spaghetti

2-3 Tbs. oil

1 Tbs. onion flakes or 1 small onion

2-4 cloves garlic or $1/4$-$1/2$ tsp. garlic powder

2 Tbs. parsley flakes

2 tsp. oregano

2 reconstituted eggs (4 Tbs. egg powder and 4 Tbs. water)

1 cup small bits of cheese (Swiss is nice here.)

HELPFUL HINTS: Cook and drain spaghetti. Sauté onion, garlic, oil and spices until tender. Add all ingredients to cooked spaghetti, stir and let it sit covered for a few minutes so the eggs will cook and cheese will melt.

STYLE POINTS: Add a cup of white wine and an 8 oz. can of whole baby clams to the sauce.

MILL VALLEY LINGUINE
(SERVES 3-4)

1 lb. linguine

$1/2$ cup dry milk

2 cups water

1 cup sun-dried tomatoes

$1/2$ cup dried mushrooms

parmesan cheese

HELPFUL HINTS: Cut tomatoes and mushrooms into smaller pieces and cover with hot water to hydrate them. Cook and drain pasta. Add milk and water and bring to a boil. Add the vegetables and whatever liquid is left. Simmer for several minutes. Add sauce to pasta. Sprinkle with parmesan cheese and pepper.

HOT OR COLD "SZECHWAN" NOODLES
(SERVES 4-5)

1 lb. spaghetti or linguine type noodles

1$\frac{1}{2}$ cups Sesame-Peanut Sauce (See Sauces)

HELPFUL HINTS: Cook and drain pasta. Prepare Hot Sesame-Peanut Sauce and stir into pasta. If you don't like hot or aren't carrying sesame oil, this is very tasty with the Peanut Butter Gravy.

STYLE POINTS: Top with scallions. For the truly brave, add cayenne.

TRULY GOURMET

LISAGNA LASAGNA
(SERVES 3-4)

$\frac{1}{2}$ cup wheat flour

$\frac{1}{2}$ cup white flour

1$\frac{1}{4}$ cups of water

2 cups pasta (elbows, shells, or spirals, etc.)

1 Tbs. baking powder (Adjust for the altitude. See Backcountry Baking.)

2 Tbs. powdered milk

2 Tbs. powdered egg

1 cup Italian Tomato Sauce (See Sauces)

$\frac{1}{4}$ lb. sliced cheese

4 cloves of garlic

$\frac{1}{2}$ onion

1 Tbs. oil

oregano

HELPFUL HINTS: Cook pasta. Sauté onion and garlic in oil. Remove from pan. In a separate pan mix flour, dry milk, egg powder, baking powder and water. Mixture should be the consistency of pancake batter. Put noodles in the bottom of the fry-bake pan and pour batter over the top. Make sauce, substituting fresh sautéed onion and garlic for recommended dry ingredients. Spread sauce over top of mixture in the pan. Cover with thin slices of cheese. Sprinkle with oregano. Stove-top bake for 20 minutes.

Thanks to Lisa Jaeger of Wyoming, Baja, Chile, Alaska, etc. She keeps threatening to stay in one place, but we don't believe her.

SMOKED SALMON PASTA
(SERVES 4)

4 garlic cloves

2 shallots

3 Tbs. butter

4 Tbs. dried tomato bits

1 env. Herb-Ox Instant Chicken Broth

8 oz. dry, smoked salmon

8 oz. angel hair pasta

$1/4$ cup capers

parmesan cheese

HELPFUL HINTS: Peel and chop garlic cloves and shallots in butter. Add dried tomato bits, chicken broth and $1/2$ cup water. Let sit 15-20 minutes. Flake salmon into garlic-tomato mix. Cook noodles and drain. Toss noodles, salmon-garlic-tomato mix, and capers. Serve sprinkled with Parmesan cheese.

Thanks to Iretta Hunter, Danville, CA.

HOT TOFU AND SESAME NOODLES
(SERVES 4)

3 packages ramen noodles

$1^1/2$ cups Hot Sesame-Peanut Sauce (See Sauces)

$1/3$ cup sesame seeds

$1/2$ cup peanuts or cashews

$1/2$ pound of tofu or 3 oz. of dried tofu

HELPFUL HINTS: Soften dried tofu by soaking in hot water for about 10 minutes. Prepare Hot Sesame-Peanut Sauce. Cook and drain ramen. Do not use flavoring packet. Combine all ingredients except peanuts/cashews. Smash these up and sprinkle them on just before serving.

STYLE POINTS: Garnish with green onions or sprouts.

VEGETABLE AND SHRIMP PASTA
(SERVES 2-4)

½ cup oil

1 lb. shrimp (fresh or canned)

2 cloves of garlic or ¼ tsp. garlic powder

2 cups of water

1 package of Knorr Vegetable Soup and Recipe Mix or equivalent

1 tsp. oregano

¼ tsp. crushed red pepper

8 oz linguine

HELPFUL HINTS: If using fresh shrimp, saute shrimp and garlic in oil until shrimp turn pink (about 5 minutes.) Remove them from pan. Add water, soup mix, oregano, and red pepper to frying pan and bring to a boil. Simmer for 5-10 minutes. Return shrimp to pan (or add canned shrimp). Warm and spoon over cooked and drained pasta.

STYLE POINTS: Use fresh shrimp. Substitute one cup of white wine for one cup of water. Works well with clams or mussels as well.

POTATOES

Harvested as early as 6000 BC. by South American Indians, this staple of the Incan Empire and the Irish was brought to the U.S. in the early 18th century. Its popularity soared around the turn of the century, and then plummeted again in the 1950's. Currently potatoes are on the upswing, but it's mostly in the French fried form. Potatoes are a nutritious, hardy addition to a backcountry menu. Unfortunately their bulk and weight turn most folks to the dried or flake options. If you can afford the space and need the weight, fresh potatoes will be tastier and healthier. They make a great addition to base camp or water-borne travel where weight is less of a consideration. If nothing else they make a great first breakfast before you hit the trail.

Dehydrated potato flakes, granules, and hash browns are widely available at super-markets. Additionally, many companies are marketing dehydrated potato and sauce mixes. Watch out for these—many are very high in fat and sodium. If you choose to buy them for the variety or ease of preparation, carefully consult the box for serving size information. A cup and a half per person is reasonable.

ESSENTIAL INSTANT POTATO FLAKES (OR PEARLS)
(SERVES 1)

⅔ cup potato flakes

2-3 Tbs. dry milk

1 glob margarine

salt and pepper to taste

⅔ cup of hot water

HELPFUL HINTS: Heat water, milk, and butter. Stir in potatoes until just moist. Let stand for 30-60 seconds. Add spices and eat.

SERVING SUGGESTIONS: Instant potato flakes or pearls are invaluable backcountry menu additions. They are an especially quick breakfast or snack before dinner, can be fried up for any meal, and make a great thickener when you put too much water in your soup. They are not good in coffee, so when you wake up gummy-eyed in the morning don't mistake them for powdered milk.

STYLE POINTS: Reconstitute potatoes with a cup of instant soup. Add chunked cheese, garlic, and chili pepper.

POPULAR VARIATIONS ON THE THEME

POTATO-NUT PATTIES

2 cups potatoes (Follow the above recipe to hydrate.)

2 cups chopped nuts (We like walnuts.)

⅓ cup melted margarine

1 Tbs. onion or chives

1 Tbs. parsley flakes

HELPFUL HINTS: Mix all ingredients together. Form into patties. Fry in oil over medium heat. You can make them without the nuts.

STYLE POINTS: Top with cheese. Melt and serve.

CHEESY POTATO CASSEROLE
(SERVES 2-4)

6 oz. dried hash brown or sliced potatoes

1⅓ cups of water

1 cup of Mustard Cheese Sauce (See Sauces)

HELPFUL HINTS: Bring water to a boil. Add potatoes and simmer until tender. Make mustard Cheese Sauce in fry-bake pan. Add potatoes, mix and bake for 15 minutes or so.

STYLE POINTS: Top with chives and sour cream.

TRULY GOURMET

SPICY SHEPHERD'S PIE
(SERVES 4-6)

About 1½-2 cups instant refried beans (or black beans) mix

2 cups instant potatoes

2 Tbs. onion flakes

1 bouillon cube or instant soup

⅓ cup dry milk

3 Tbs. margarine

1 cup freeze-dried corn

1 cup cheese cut into small bits

Salt, pepper and Tabasco to taste

HELPFUL HINTS: Combine 2 cups of hot water with milk, margarine, and bouillon cube. Set aside. In the bottom of your fry-bake pan, combine 2-3 cups of boiling water with corn and beans. Simmer until corn is tender and beans hydrated. Remove from heat. Spread patties over beans, add salt, pepper, and Tabasco. Top with cheese. Stovetop bake until hot and cheese melts (about 15 minutes).

STYLE POINTS: Substitute a cup of dried ground beef or sausage for half of the beans. Top with sour cream.

GRAPENUT SURPRISE
(aka POWER LOAD DINNER)
(SERVES 3-4)

2 cups potato flakes

2 cups instant refried beans

2 cups cheddar cheese

2 cups Grapenuts

¼ cup margarine

black pepper, chili pepper, cayenne, garlic powder to taste

HELPFUL HINTS: Boil 2 pots of water with 2 cups of water in each. Hydrate potato and refried beans in separate pots. Mix chili pepper, pepper and cayenne into beans to taste. Be careful if you bought refrieds that already have been spiced. Set both aside. Melt margarine in bottom of fry-bake pan. Add ⅔ of the Grapenuts until they are saturated with fat. Remove from heat and smash into a crust. Cover crust with a layer of sliced cheddar. Add a layer of potatoes and a layer of beans. Top with a final layer of cheese and sprinkle with Grapenuts, garlic and chili powder. Stove-top bake until the cheese has melted (about 10-15 minutes.)

Thanks to Shana Tarter and Steve Platz, Ithaca, NY. They needed this on their honeymoon.

SIMPLE POTATO CURRY
(SERVES 2)

2 cups dried hash brown potatoes

1⅓ cups of water

2-3 Tbs. margarine

1-2 tsp. curry powder

½ tsp. garlic powder

HELPFUL HINTS: Fry all ingredients together until water is absorbed and potatoes are tender.

STYLE POINTS: Top with sour cream.

BEANS: THE MUSICAL FRUIT

Actually, beans aren't fruit at all. They're all dried seeds from leguminous plants. Each bean (legume) has a characteristic flavor and texture, and all beans are excellent sources of protein when combined with grains, seeds, or small amounts of milk, cheese, or meat. The problem with beans in the backcountry is not the snide remarks from your traveling companions but the time they take to cook. A pot of legumes can take from 20 minutes (lentils) to 3 ½ hours (chickpeas) to soften to the point that they are edible. Don't let this discourage you, just choose carefully. Lentils and split peas make wonderful backcountry meals and many beans, such as pintos and black beans, can be purchased in quick-cooking styles. Soaking and pressure-cooking beans can cut down on the cooking time as well. And don't forget that falafel and NatureBurger are also bean by-products. Bean dishes are widely available in pre-packaged forms from supermarkets, health food stores and outdoor retailers. Below are some dishes you can easily throw together yourself.

ESSENTIAL LENTIL RECIPE
(SERVES 2)

1 cup lentils

3 cups water

¼ tsp. salt

HELPFUL HINTS: Cover with water and bring to a boil. Cover and simmer for 20-40 minutes until tender. Although presoaking is not required, we find it cuts down on the cooking time. Carry them soaking in a water bottle while you hike or paddle.

SERVING SUGGESTIONS: Top with Curry Sauce. (See Sauces)

ESSENTIAL INSTANT REFRIED BEAN OR BLACK BEANS RECIPE
(SERVES 2)

1 cup instant beans

¾-1 cup water

1-2 Tbs. margarine

HELPFUL HINTS: If you have bean flakes, you can add the margarine and boiling water to beans and set it aside while it hydrates (5-10 minutes). At altitude or if you have dried whole beans, some limited simmering may be required. If your beans are not pre-spiced, add salt, pepper, chili powder and cumin to taste.

SERVING SUGGESTIONS: Top with cheese and use a tortilla as a spoon.

STYLE POINTS: Serve with sour cream and sprouts.

ESSENTIAL FALAFEL RECIPE
(SERVES 2)

1 cup falafel
¾ cup water
oil for frying

HELPFUL HINTS: Mix with water and let it stand. Form into thin patties (1/2 inch) and fry in oil. Don't squish them with the spatula while they're in the pan or they will break apart. This is fragile business.

SERVING SUGGESTIONS: Top with a slice of cheese, roll in a tortilla, sprinkle on the Tabasco and eat. Falafel burgers are also delicious with many of this book's sauces (See Sauces).

STYLE POINTS: Form into meatball-sized rounds and serve with Italian spaghetti. We call this spaghetti and falafel balls.

POPULAR VARIATIONS ON THE BEAN THEME

LENTIL CHILI
(SERVES 3-4)

1½ cups lentils ₂ ¼
4-5 cups water 6
4 Tbs. tomato powder 6
1-2 Tbs. onion flakes 3
1 Tbs. chili powder or more to taste. 1,5
1 tsp. cumin

1 tsp. oregano 2

1 tsp. garlic powder 2

2 Tbs. cornmeal   3

black and red pepper to taste

cheddar cheese

HELPFUL HINTS: Combine water and lentils and bring to a boil. Add all ingredients and simmer until done. Serve and top with cheese chunks.

STYLE POINTS: Add dried peppers, corn or tomatoes to the chili. Serve over corn bread.

CURRIED LENTILS
(SERVES 3-4)

1 cup lentils

3 cups of water

1-2 Tbs. onion flakes

1-2 tsp. curry powder

1 vegetable bouillon cube

1 cup chopped dried fruit

$1/2$ cup sunflower seeds or other suitable nut

$1/3$ cup coconut (optional)

HELPFUL HINTS: Bring water, lentils, and bouillon cube to a boil. When water is half absorbed add fruit and spices. Simmer until lentils are tender. Add nuts and coconut and serve.

STYLE POINTS: Use a mixture of lentils and rice, or bulgur and rice.

LENTIL PILAF
(SERVES 3-4)

$^1/_2$ cup lentils

$^1/_2$ cup rice

$2^1/_2$-3 cups water

1-2 pkg. of instant soup (cream of chicken or tomato works well.)

1 cup dried carrots

2 Tbs. margarine

4-6 Tbs. dried red and green peppers

2 Tbs. onion flakes

1 tsp. cumin

$^1/_2$ tsp. basil

$^1/_2$ tsp. garlic powder

HELPFUL HINTS: Boil water, add all ingredients and simmer until tender.

STYLE POINTS: After everything is tender, fry the pilaf in margarine. Top it with cheese and nuts. Melt and serve.

SWEET AND SOUR LENTILS
(SERVES 3-4)

1 cup of lentils

3 cups of water

$^1/_4$ cup red and green peppers

$^1/_4$ cup raisins

$^1/_4$ cup pineapple chunks or chopped apricots

3 Tbs. soy sauce

$^1/_4$ cup dried carrots

1 pkg. of sweet and sour mix

HELPFUL HINTS: Pour hot water over dried fruit and vegetables. Cook lentils. Add package to fruit and vegetable mix return to a boil. Pour over lentils, mix and serve.

STYLE POINTS: Serve with almonds or combine with pasta for a larger group.

LENTIL PATTIES
(SERVES 3-4)

1 cup lentils

1 cup bulgur

3-4 cups water

$1/2$ tsp. garlic powder

1 Tbs. parsley flakes

1 Tbs. onion flakes

2 Tbs. oil

$1/4$ tsp. black pepper

$1/4$ cup flour

HELPFUL HINTS: Combine onions, garlic, lentils and 3-4 cups of water. Simmer for 20-25 minutes. Add bulgur, parsley, oil, and spices. Simmer until tender. Mash and mix in flour. If for some reason the mixture is too thin to form patties add more flour or corn meal. Form into patties, crisp in buttered fry pan.

STYLE POINTS: Serve topped with Peanut Sauce (See Sauces).

TRULY GOURMET

ENCHILADA PIE
(SERVES 4)

3 10-inch (or the size of your baking pan) flour tortillas

2 cups dried instant refried beans

$1^{1}/2$ cups Mexican Sauce (See Sauces)

$1/4$ cup red and green peppers

1 cup dried corn

2 cups cheese cut into slices

1 package sour cream mix

HELPFUL HINTS: Add $2^{1}/2$ -3 cups of boiling water to beans and vegetables. Cover and set aside. Put together the sauce. Pour $1/3$ of sauce in the bottom of deep dish fry pan. Alternate three layers of tortillas, beans, and cheese. Spread remaining sauce on top. Stove-top bake for 20-30 minutes. Top with sour cream and serve.

PIZZA
(SERVES 2)

Pizza is a quick and easy dinner that consistently amazes your friends and, sometimes, even your enemies. All you need is a deep dish frying pan with a lid and the courage to try. Below you will find some crusts of varying intensity of commitment, plus some traditional and not so traditional toppings.

BOTTOMS

(THESE CRUSTS FIT A 9-10 INCH DEEP DISH PAN.)

SUPER-QUICK CRUST

If you have a low commitment level, for the quickest pizza-like meal, heat your frying pan and one side of a tortilla or pita bread, flip it over, add the toppings and the lid until the cheese melts and you're eating a pizza-like treat in less than ten minutes.

QUICK PIZZA CRUST

¾ cup Essential Batter Mix (See Backcountry Baking)

¾ cup flour

½ cup water

1 Tbs. oil

HELPFUL HINTS: Mix into a stiff dough. Oil bottom of fry-bake pan. Press dough firmly into bottom of pan. For a low commitment level, flip-bake the crust about 10 minutes a side. (Add toppings after the flip!) If you have the time, add toppings and stovetop bake for higher style points.

STYLE POINTS: Add 1-2 tsp. of Italian seasoning to the dough before mixing in the water.

THE "REAL THING" PIZZA CRUST

1 Tbs. dry yeast

1 Tbs. sugar or honey

1/4 tsp. salt

1 1/2 cups flour

About 2/3-3/4 cup lukewarm water

HELPFUL HINTS: Combine yeast, sugar, and water in an insulated mug. When yeast froths to the top combine slowly with flour and salt stirring at first and then kneading until the dough is smooth. Put in a warm place to double in size. Knead again until dough is smooth. Press into bottom of oiled pan, add toppings and stove-top bake about 20-30 minutes.

(For more help on yeast and baking in general see Backcountry Baking.)

TOPS

TRADITIONAL LID

3/4 cup Italian Tomato Sauce (See Sauces)

1 cup mozzarella cheese

veggies of your choice

parmesan cheese

HELPFUL HINTS: Top crust of your choice with sauce, hydrated vegetables, and cheese. Bake by preferred method.

HERB LID

1 cup of Cheese Sauce (See Sauces)

1/2-1 Tbs. of basil, chives, sage, or rosemary (or a combination)

HELPFUL HINTS: Top crust of your choice and bake by preferred method.

MEAT LOVERS LID

1 cup of Italian Tomato Sauce

or

1 cup Tomato Cream Sauce (See Sauces)

1 cup cheese cut into small bits

1 cup sliced sausage or pepperoni

HELPFUL HINTS: Top crust of your choice with sauce, meat and finally cheese. Bake by preferred method.

VEGETARIAN LID

1 cup Italian Tomato Sauce (See Sauces)

1-2 cups of dried vegetables (peppers and mushrooms work well)

1 cup of cheese cut into small bits

HELPFUL HINTS: Top crust of your choice with sauce, hydrated vegetables and cheese. Bake by preferred method.

STYLE POINTS: Substitute tomato sauce for cream sauce. Sprinkle with sunflower seeds.

TRUSTAFERRIAN LID

1 cup Alfredo Sauce (See Sauces)

1 cup dried mushrooms

1 cup sun-dried tomatoes

parmesan cheese and crushed red pepper to taste

HELPFUL HINTS: Top your crust of choice with sauce, hydrated mushrooms and tomatoes. Bake by preferred method. Let folks sprinkle the parmesan, and especially the red pepper, themselves . . . if you like them.

STYLE POINTS: Top with sprouts.

HOT TO TROT LID

1 cup Mexican Sauce (See Sauces)

1 cup freeze-dried corn

1 cup cheddar cheese cut into small bits

Tabasco to taste

HELPFUL HINTS: Top crust of your choice with sauce, hydrated corn, and cheese. (Goes well with Pan Cornbread. See Backcountry Baking.) Bake by preferred method.

STYLE POINTS: Add a cup of meat, lentils, or beans to sauce.

Backcountry Baking

S urely this was a dream. Breakfast deep in the backcountry takes on an unappealing familiarity: cold granola, sticky oatmeal, something unidentifiable dumped
into lukewarm water in hopes it will dissolve completely before you try to swallow it. But this cold Wind River morning, waiting for the sun to crawl over the ridge
before I crawled out of the bag, friendly aromas sat me up under the sheltering tarp.
There was fresh coffee and, yes, the warm smell of baking yeast and . . . what was it?

She looked up from the whispering stove and smiled. "Let's go. Cinnamon rolls are
almost ready."

Served hot, the melting butter dribbled over my fingers. "Great! Wonderful!
Terrific!" I searched futilely for descriptives, knowing I had found a backpacking part-
ner I didn't want to lose. That was over a decade ago, and we're still baking together.
The longer the trip, the more we appreciate these freshly baked changes in diet.

OPTION 1: STOVE-TOP BAKING

THE TOOLS

You will need one deep ($1\frac{1}{2}$ -2") non-stick fry-bake pan with a lid that fits snugly. Your
batter or dough should not over-fill the pan. Half-full is a good gauge or the rising that
ensues when you bake causes the batter to overflow or minimally stick to the lid. The
lid must fit tightly to ensure that you adequately trap the required amount of heat. If
your pan is smaller than this, merely cut the recipes in half and proceed as directed.
We like the large pan even for the two of us because if you are going to the trouble to
bake it's rewarding to have leftovers. OK, we're pigs.

THE HEAT

You will need a source of bottom heat. In this case, a backpacking stove that simmers
well. In preparation for Stove-Top baking, light your chosen stove and adjust it to a
simmer. You should be able to hold your hand comfortably about 10 inches above the
stove, but still feel your hand being warmed. Too hot is generally more of a problem
than too cold.

Equally as important as bottom heat is a source of top heat. Traditionally, this is where you build a small, hot twiggy fire on top of your lid. Recently, we have discovered the Pot Parka, a convection dome marketed by Traveling Light. We will discuss both options.

STOVE-TOP BAKING WITH THE TWIGGY FIRE

Gather a pile of pencil-sized or smaller twigs. Light your stove and let it run at its lowest heat. Put the baking pan, with secure lid, on the stove, and build a twiggy fire on the lid. Spread the fire out evenly on the lid, and feed it enough wood to keep it burn-

ing. It's almost impossible to produce too much heat on the lid. Every 4 to 5 minutes rotate the pan clockwise to assure even baking on the bottom. Use a couple of sticks to make rotating the pan simple and painless. Total cooking time usually runs 30 to 40 minutes. After 20 to 30 minutes, or if you start to smell the rich aroma, carefully lift off the lid and check the progress, just to be safe. DON'T LIFT THE LID TOO OFTEN, or you will keep losing the heat needed to bake the goodie. When the dough is cooked, it has a firm crust and sounds hollow when you thump it. Set the pan off the stove, but continue to burn the twiggy fire on top until nothing is left except a fine ash that can be scattered harmlessly.

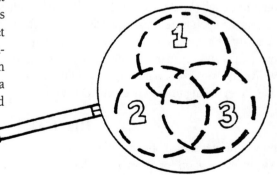

THE PAN IS MOVED SO THAT THE HEAT SOURCE IS MOVED THROUGH THE THREE LOCATIONS EVENLY.

STOVE-TOP BAKING WITH THE CONVECTION DOME

This item has revolutionized our Stove-Top baking. Follow the directions for baking with a twiggy fire only skip the twiggies. The convection dome, or Pot Parka, surrounds the fry-bake pan trapping all the heat around and on top of the pan. You have a light-weight mini-oven! Although the twiggy fire works great, the convection dome cuts down on baking time (about 30%), and the chance of fire. It folds neatly into the pan for travel. We love it and go nowhere without it. (OK, maybe a couple of places.) Basically, what you're doing is converting your pan into the Outback Oven (See Gear for the Outdoor Kitchen).

OPTION 2: FLIP-BAKING

Flip-baking is faster. You end up with a still tasty yet denser version of your stove-top baked bread. It is useful if you are in a rush, you forgot your convection dome (heaven forbid), the twiggy supply in the area is low, or the fire danger is high. Merely oil your fry-bake pan, place the dough or batter inside, and flip carefully when it is done on one side. Cook until both sides are toasty and the middle is not gooey. Time per side depends on thickness of the dough and the heat of the stove. To prevent "black on the outside, goo on the inside", flip-bake over medium heat with the lid in place. We traditionally flip-bake pancakes, pan biscuits, chapatis, tortillas, johnnycakes, and many other things when we're too hungry to wait.

ESSENTIAL BATTER MIX

The initial Essential Batter Mix ingredients will vary little from pancakes to quick breads to pie crust. What will vary is the consistency of the batter and the additional ingredients (the ingredients that make it special). For example, pancake batter needs to be lumpless and pour easily; muffins and cakes need to be thicker but still pour if you encourage it; and biscuit dough needs to be just that, dough (sticky, but you can form it into a ball and it stays there). So these recipes will include some ideas about amounts of fluid needed, but the best plan is to add water slowly until the batter is the desired consistency.

B2's ESSENTIAL BATTER MIX

2 cups flour

$^1/_3$ - $^1/_2$ cup dry milk

4 tsp. baking powder

$^1/_2$ cup margarine or shortening

$^1/_2$ tsp. salt (optional)

Water

HOW MUCH WATER?

For Pancake Batter: About 2 cups. Batter should run off spoon easily.

For Cake Batter: About 1$^1/_2$-1$^3/_4$ cups. Batter should walk off spoon quickly.

For Muffin/Quick Bread Batter: About 1$^1/_4$-1$^1/_2$ cups. Batter should drop off spoon into pan, but it's not in a huge rush. This batter is about twice as thick as pancakes.

For Biscuit Batter: About 3/4 cup. This batter is quite stiff but still sticky. You definitely have to push it of the spoon or press it into a pan. It will not go anywhere by itself.

IMPORTANT: ALTITUDE ADJUSTMENTS!

The thing that does seriously affect baking is the altitude at which you are cooking. The higher you go, the less leavening agent (baking powder) you will need. So when making your Essential Batter Mix, either at home or on the trail, think about your altitude and adjust your ingredients appropriately. Also, buy double-acting baking powder. It releases its leavening in two stages so cakes won't rise too fast.

If you do not adjust for the altitude your baked goods will expand out of your pan, crumble into a small pile and be otherwise inedible without rolling them into crumb balls or eating them with a spoon.

BAKING POWDER: Use double-acting.

0-3500 feet: Use 4 tsp. per 2 cups of flour.

3500-6500: Use 3$^1/_2$ tsp. per 2 cups of flour.

6500-8500: Use 3 tsp. per 2 cups of flour.

8500-10,000: Use 2$^1/_2$ tsp. per 2 cups of flour.

Over 10,000: Use 2 tsp. and an extra egg (2 Tbs. powdered egg) per 2 cups of flour.

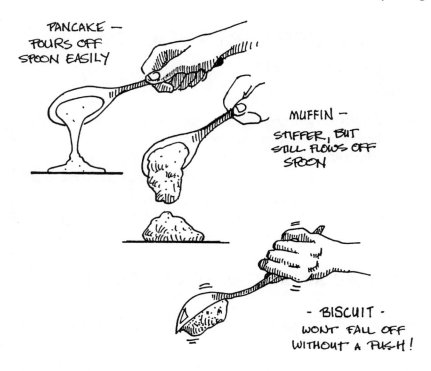

PANCAKE — POURS OFF SPOON EASILY

MUFFIN — STIFFER, BUT STILL FLOWS OFF SPOON

- BISCUIT - WONT FALL OFF WITHOUT A PUSH!

There are more exact adjustments, but this works. If the recipe calls for a lot of sugar, many people cut it back a tablespoon or two as they gain elevation. We don't usually worry about it, but using too much sugar at the higher altitudes may make your cakes fall by destroying their cell structure.

COMMERCIAL MIXES

Commercial mixes are prepared for sea level, in fact most have altitude adjustments on the packaging. We found this out when we built our cabin at 9200 feet. Your cake mixes expand like a bad horror movie all over the oven. To combat this dilemma, you must add extra flour to the mixes. Also, add some extra water to compensate for the extra flour and the fact that water evaporates faster at these drier heights. Please don't be overwhelmed. Use the guidelines below to adjust your commercial mixes before baking.

For every two cups of mix add:

3500-6500 feet: 2 Tbs. each flour and water.

6500-8500 feet: 3 Tbs. each flour and water.

8500-10,000 feet: 4 Tbs. (1/4 cup) each flour and water.

Above 10,000 feet: 4 Tbs. (1/4 cup) each flour and water and an extra egg.

ESSENTIAL PAN BISCUITS

2 cups Essential Batter Mix

3/4 cup water

HELPFUL HINTS: Mix wet with dry ingredients. Form into a ball. Knead lightly (about 30 seconds). Pinch off balls of dough and form into patties (1/2" thick) and fry in buttered fry pan a few minutes a side.

STYLE POINTS: Serve smothered in syrup or gravy (See Breakfasts and/or Sauces).

Thanks to Ardath Drown Gray and Elsie Emmons Cummings who had the courage to teach a small girl how to make biscuits and let her practice. "Cut the shortening with your hands. It's the only way they come out right."

POPULAR VARIATIONS ON THE THEME

BUTTERMILK BISCUITS: Make the Essential Batter with buttermilk powder and proceed as in Pan Biscuits.

BACON BISCUITS: Add 1/3 cup bacon bits to Essential Pan Biscuits and proceed as above.

CHEESE AND GARLIC BISCUITS: Add 1/2 cup grated cheese and 1/2 tsp. garlic powder to Essential Pan Biscuits.

HERB BISCUITS: Add 1/2 tsp. dry mustard, 1/2 tsp. sage and 1 1/4 tsp. caraway seeds to Essential Pan Biscuits. Other herbs work well too.

SIN-A-MON BISCUITS: See Breakfasts.

PSEUDOSCONES: See Breakfasts.

TRULY GOURMET

TILTON'S TRAVELING OAT CAKES

2 1/4 cups white flour

1 cup wheat flour

3/4 cup oatmeal

1 tsp. salt

$^1\!/_2$ cup sugar

2 tsp. baking powder

2 Tbs. dry milk

1 tsp. cinnamon

$^1\!/_2$ cup oil

about 1 cup water

HELPFUL HINTS: Bring oil, sugar, dry milk and water to a boil. Stir until sugar is dissolved and remove from heat. Combine dry ingredients, add sugary milk mixture and stir until all ingredients are moist. Shape dough into round biscuits $^1\!/_2$" thick x 3" diameter and flip-bake as described in Essential Pan Biscuits.

STYLE POINTS: Pull these out at lunch and serve with cheese, jam or peanut butter.

JAM JEWELS

2 cups Essential Batter Mix

$^3\!/_4$ cup water

Jam or Wild Berry Syrup (See Breakfasts)

HELPFUL HINTS: Follow mixing directions of Essential Pan Biscuits. Form dough into patties approximately 3 inches in diameter and $^1\!/_4$ inch thick. Drop a spoonful of jelly or thick Berry Syrup in the middle. Fold over and pinch edges tightly shut. If you have trouble sealing dough, dab a little water on the edge. Flip-bake in margarine or snuggle them into the bottom of your pan and stove-top bake.

QUICK BREADS

SPEEDY BANNOCK:
A Simple Mountain Bread
(MAKES ONE 10" ROUND)

2 cups Essential Batter Mix (We like $^1\!/_2$ white/$^1\!/_2$ wheat.)

1 cup of water

HELPFUL HINTS: Mix dry with wet ingredients. Place or press in oiled fry-bake pan. stove-top or flip-bake until done.

STYLE POINTS: Add cinnamon, sugar, and raisins.

HERBS AND CHEESE QUICK BREAD

1 Speedy Bannock Batter

1 tsp. garlic powder

1 tsp. basil or oregano or Italian spices

1/4 cup parmesan or romano cheese

HELPFUL HINTS: Combine all ingredients and proceed as in Speedy Bannock.

CORNBREAD
(MAKES ONE 10" ROUND)

1 cup cornmeal

1 cup flour

1/2 tsp. salt (optional)

1 Tbs. sugar

2 Tbs. egg powder

2 tsp. baking powder

1 Tbs. oil or melted margarine

1/4 cup buttermilk powder

1 1/3 cups water

HELPFUL HINTS: Combine all ingredients until they are just wet. For Traditional Johnnycake, divide the batter into two to three portions and flip-bake in a fry pan. For cornbread stove-top bake.

STYLE POINTS: Add 1 cup of hydrated corn and/or 1 cup cheese bits. For crunchy cornbread, add 1/4 cup sunflower seeds to the batter.

HUSH PUPPIES

1 cup cornmeal

$\frac{1}{2}$ cup white flour

1 Tbs. sugar

$2\frac{1}{2}$ tsp. baking powder

2 Tbs. egg powder

1 Tbs. onion flakes

3 Tbs. buttermilk powder

salt to taste

about $\frac{3}{4}$ cup water

HELPFUL HINTS: Mix all ingredients together thoroughly. Put a liberal amount of oil into a frying pan. Drop by spoonful (or shape into patties) into hot oil and fry until they are brown. These are traditionally deep-fried, but you can get away with a lot less oil by turning them frequently.

CHAPATIS
(MAKES 12)

2 cups of whole wheat flour

$\frac{3}{4}$ cup water

$\frac{1}{2}$ tsp. salt (optional)

2 Tbs. oil

HELPFUL HINTS: Mix all ingredients and knead until dough is smooth. Pinch off about 12 small balls of equal size. Pat balls into thin patties between your hands until they are very thin. Drop the flattened dough into a hot frying pan. Cook on one side until brown and flip. Cook second side. About 2 minutes a side.

FLOUR TORTILLAS
(MAKES 12)

2 cups of white flour

$1\frac{1}{2}$ Tbs. shortening or margarine

1 tsp. baking powder

$\frac{3}{4}$ cup cold water

$\frac{1}{2}$ tsp. salt (optional)

HELPFUL HINTS: Mix dry ingredients and cut in margarine with a spoon. (We usually blend it in with our washed hands.) Add the water slowly until you have a stiff dough. Divide the dough into 12 balls. Roll them out very thin between 2 plastic bags. Use your water bottle as a rolling pin. Flip-bake about 2 minutes a side.

QUICK SWEET BREAD

2 cups Essential Batter Mix

$\frac{1}{4}$-$\frac{1}{2}$ cup sugar

2 Tbs. egg powder

$1\frac{1}{2}$ cups water

HELPFUL HINTS: Combine dry ingredients and stir in wet. Do not over mix. Pour into oiled fry-bake pan and stove-top bake until done. About 20-30 minutes.

POPULAR VARIATIONS ON THE THEME

FRUIT SWEET BREAD

Add 1 cup of chopped dried fruit (We like apples and raisins, but mixed fruit works well, or just raisins.) and $\frac{1}{2}$ tsp. of cinnamon to the Quick Sweet Bread recipe above. Hydrate fruit with hot water before adding it to mixture.

WILD BERRY BREAD

Add 1 cup of wild berries and proceed as above.

OATMEAL QUICK BREAD

Substitute 1 cup of oats for 1 cup of Basic Batter Mix. Add ½ cup of raisins and ½ tsp. cinnamon.

COFFEECAKES: See Breakfasts.

TRULY GOURMET

APRICOT BREAD

1½ cups Essential Batter Mix

½ cup Grapenuts

⅔ cup dried chopped apricots

½ cup sugar

2 Tbs. egg powder

1¼ -1½ cups water

HELPFUL HINTS: Pour boiling water over the apricots. Combine all dry ingredients and mix in wet. Add hydrated apricots. Pour into oiled fry-bake pan and stove-top bake until done. About 20-30 minutes.

STYLE POINTS: Add ½ cup chopped nuts. Pecans are nice.

BACKCOUNTRY CARROT BREAD

2 cups Essential Batter Mix or any commercial baking mix

½ cup dry milk

½ cup brown sugar

1 tsp. cinnamon

1 grated carrot

1 handful of raisins

¾-1 cup water

HELPFUL HINTS: Combine batter mix, dry milk, sugar and cinnamon. Gently add carrot, raisins and water. Mix until all ingredients are wet and press into the bottom of fry-bake pan. Flip-bake on low heat until done.

Thanks to J. Scott McGee, Redmond, OR.

PEANUT BUTTER BREAD

2 cups flour
4 tsp. baking powder
1/3 cup sugar
3/4 cup peanut butter
1/2 cup dry milk
2 Tbs. egg powder
1 1/3 cup water

HELPFUL HINTS: Combine all dry ingredients. Cut in peanut butter with two knives or forks until the mixture is crumbly. Add water and mix all ingredients thoroughly. Pour into oiled fry-bake pan and stove-top bake until done. About 30-40 minutes.

GRAPENUT BREAD

1 1/2 cups flour
1 1/4 cup Grapenuts
1/4 cup brown sugar
2 Tbs. egg powder
1 1/2 tsp. baking powder
1/4 tsp. salt
1/2 tsp. cinnamon
3 Tbs. margarine
1/4 cup dry milk
about 1 1/4 cups water

Helpful Hints: Sauté the Grapenuts in margarine for about 5 minutes. Remove from heat add sugar. Beat together the egg powder, dry milk and water. Add the Grapenuts. Mix all the remaining dry ingredients and mix with the wet. Stove-top bake in oiled fry-bake pan until done. About 20-30 minutes.

YEAST BREADS

Yeast . . . something that sometimes makes bread rise, a source of fear and loathing, certainly not to be considered when packing for the wilderness. Wait a minute. . .Why not? Yeast wants to be your friend.

Yeast is a colony of minute fungi, living organisms, sleeping as dried flakes, powder, or cake. Warm water is needed to wake it up, and sugar is required to feed it while it grows. Yeast causes dough to rise by forming tiny pockets of carbon dioxide secondary to the fermentation of the sugar. Water should be very warm but not hot (you should be able to hold your finger in it, but just barely), and the sugar can be white, brown, molasses, honey, whatever you choose.

ESSENTIAL YEAST BREAD

1 pkg. yeast (1 Tbs.)

2 Tbs. sugar

1 tsp. salt (optional)

1¼ cups warm water

2 Tbs. oil or melted margarine (optional)

3 cups flour

HELPFUL HINTS: Combine the warm water, yeast and sugar. (Some people like to add a teaspoon of salt and one or two tablespoons of oil. Some people don't.) We let the yeast begin its life in a pre-warmed plastic, insulated mug to hold the heat. In about 5-10 minutes, the mass in the mug starts to bubble out the top, the yeast is fully awake and ready to use. Yeast is fragile during the first few minutes of awakening, and it will die if it gets too cold . . . or too hot. But once it's mixed with flour, it grows strong and hard-to-kill.

Put about 2 cups of flour in a pot, and add the activated yeast mixture. We like to mix wheat and white flour 50-50. Beat the mixture together with a spoon for 3 to 4 minutes, until it becomes a stringy mess. Add more flour slowly, kneading it into the mixture. Kneading can be done in the pot, in a fry pan, on a plastic bag, or on a foam-lite sleeping pad, wherever it's convenient. Keep adding flour and kneading until a non-sticky ball of dough, that holds its shape, is formed. Total flour used will probably be about 3 cups.

Don't worry too much about your kneading style. We use the palms of our hands folding the dough towards us and then turning the ends on top when it starts to get too narrow to comfortably work it. Basically, dough likes a firm massage so come up with your own method.

Plop the kneaded dough in a well-oiled, covered pot and set it in the sun to rise. If it's cold, we oil the surface of the doughball, put it in two plastic bags, and wear it inside our clothing until it rises. For fresh rolls in the morning, whip up the doughball at night, double-bag it, and sleep with it.

If you're in a hurry, dough doesn't have to rise to be used. The heat of baking will cause some rising. But the more it rises, the lighter and less dense the final product will be.

Before baking, knead the dough again for a few minutes, and place it in a well-oiled fry-bake pan. Stove-top bake, for a lighter yeast bread, or flip-bake, for a denser bread.

Style Points: Divide and roll your dough into snakes, then spiral, twist or braid the snakes around your pan. Practice your knots with the snakes and bake them that way. For rolls pinch off bits of the dough, roll them into balls, and pack them tightly into your fry-bake pan.

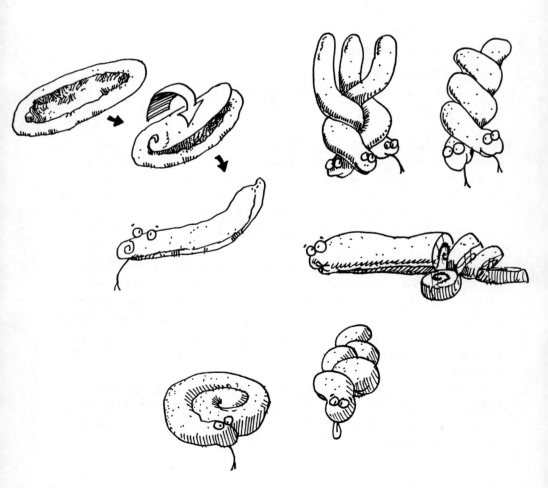

POPULAR VARIATIONS TO THE THEME

NUTRITION BOOST: Add 2-4 Tbs. egg powder and $\frac{1}{2}$ cup dry milk to dry ingredients. Substitute $\frac{1}{2}$ cup wheat germ or bran for $\frac{1}{2}$ cup flour.

FRUIT AND NUT BREAD: Add handful of dried chopped fruit and nuts, to dough before adding final cup of flour.

VEGETABLE BREAD: Add 1 Tbs. hydrated onion flakes, $\frac{1}{2}$ tsp. garlic powder, $\frac{1}{2}$ Tbs. parsley, and $\frac{1}{2}$ cup hydrated smashed up vegetables. Use a packet of bouillon instead of salt. Black pepper to taste. A handful of sunflower seeds are nice in this one too.

MULTI-GRAIN BREAD: Substitute $\frac{1}{2}$ cup cooked grain for $\frac{1}{2}$ cup flour. This is a great way to get rid of left-overs.

CHILI BREAD: Add 1 tsp. chili powder, 1 tsp. basil, and $\frac{1}{4}$ tsp. garlic and cayenne. Top with cheese and/or beans.

RAISIN OATMEAL BREAD: Substitute $\frac{1}{2}$ cup cooked oatmeal for $\frac{1}{2}$ cup flour. Add $\frac{1}{2}$ cup raisins and $\frac{1}{2}$ tsp. cinnamon.

TRULY GOURMET

SWEET CINNAMON BREAD

1 Essential Yeast Bread dough

2 tsp. cinnamon

$\frac{1}{2}$ cup brown sugar

handful of raisins

handful of nuts

HELPFUL HINTS: Proceed with Basic Yeast Bread recipe but, before you add the last cup of flour, add the extra ingredients.

Thanks to J. Scott McGee, Redmond, OR.

GARLIC HERB BREAD

1 Essential Yeast Bread dough

2 Tbs. herbs (oregano, basil, Italian, parsley, etc.)

2 cloves fresh garlic or 1 tsp. garlic powder

HELPFUL HINTS: Sauté garlic and herbs lightly in melted butter. Let cool and add before blending in last cup of flour. Proceed as in Essential Yeast Bread.

STYLE POINTS: Add ½ cup of parmesan to dry ingredients. Just before you're ready to bake, press chunks of Swiss cheese into the dough about an inch apart. Stove-top bake.

Thanks to J. Scott McGee, Redmond, OR.

Desserts

NO COOKING REQUIRED DESSERTS

PUDDING
(SERVES 2)

1 instant pudding mix

1/2 cup dry milk

2 cups cold water

HELPFUL HINTS: Don't add too much water. We like to shake the mix in a water bottle (45 seconds) or whisk it (1-2 minutes) and then secure it in a stream or snow bank to thicken. Makes a great rich shake or cake topping, too.

STYLE POINTS: Add leftover rice to pudding.

SNOW SHAKE

2 Tbs. egg powder

1/4 cup dry milk

1 Tbs. sugar

1 tsp. vanilla

1 cup water

HELPFUL HINTS: Combine above ingredients thoroughly and add snow until mixture is thick and creamy.

STYLE POINTS: Leave out the sugar and add 2-3 Tbs. hot chocolate, pudding, or cheesecake mix.

SNOW CONES

#1: Mix fruit drink crystals or apple cider mix into a syrup. Pour over a mug of snow.

#2: Sprinkle fruit flavored gelatin over a mug of snow.

#3. Mix a mug full of snow with any of the syrups (See Breakfasts).

LIMITED COOKING REQUIRED DESSERTS

CHOCOLATE FONDUE

2 cups dry chocolate frosting mix

1 tsp. instant coffee or cinnamon and cloves to taste

4 Tbs. margarine

1 Tbs. dry milk

3 Tbs. water

HELPFUL HINTS: Melt margarine and combine all ingredients. Heat until hot but not boiling.

SERVING SUGGESTIONS: Dip with sweet bread, cake, graham crackers, vanilla wafers, marshmallows, fruit, or anything else you can find.

ALMOST PEANUT BUTTER CUPS
(MAKES 1 10" ROUND)

3/4 cup graham cracker or cookie crumbs

3/4 cup peanut butter (crunchy is better)

1/2 pound powdered sugar

1/4 cup margarine

1 1/2 cups chocolate chips

HELPFUL HINTS: Melt margarine and mix in peanut butter, sugar, crumbs. Press into bottom of fry-bake pan. Melt chips and pour them over crust. Chill for and hour or so, if you can wait that long.

Style Points go to Tilda Musgrove, Live Oak, FL.

NO BAKE PIE
(MAKES ONE 10" PIE)

CRUST:

1 cup graham cracker crumbs

3 Tbs. sugar

1/3 cup melted margarine

FILLING:

1 instant pudding mix

1/2 cup dry milk

2 cups water

HELPFUL HINTS: You can buy Oreo, graham cracker or ginger snap crumbs in the baking section of most supermarkets, or just carry them in your pack for a few days and let the job do itself. Melt margarine and combine it with the crumbs and sugar. If you're using cookie crumbs, leave out the sugar. Press mixture into the bottom of a fry pan. Make pudding in a bowl, or we like to shake it in a water bottle. Pour over crust and set aside to chill.

FAVORITE COMBINATIONS:

#1: Oreo crumbs and milk chocolate pudding

#2: Ginger snap crumbs and tapioca

#3: Graham cracker crumbs and banana or coconut pudding

CHEESECAKE OR CHOCOLATE MOUSSE PIE
(MAKES ONE 8"-10" PIE)

These mixes are commercially available packaged with directions and crust, but here's some general guidelines if you buy bulk or lose the directions.

CRUST: Mix crumbs with 3 Tbs. melted margarine. Press crumbs firmly into bottom of the pan. We like to sprinkle them on the top of filling for a quick, non-frustrating option.

FILLING: Mix filling (about 1 cup) with 1/2 cup dry milk and about 1 1/2 cups cold water. Beat with whisk or spoon until thick. Place on crust, cover and set aside to chill.

STYLE POINTS: Top cheesecake with berry syrup.

MAINE NO-BAKE COOKIES
(SERVES 4-6)

3 cups quick oats

$\frac{1}{2}$ cup margarine

$\frac{1}{2}$ cup peanut butter

2 Tbs. dry milk

$\frac{1}{2}$ cup water

2 cups sugar

3 Tbs. cocoa

1 cup chopped nuts (optional)

HELPFUL HINTS: Bring margarine, milk, water, sugar and cocoa to a boil. Remove from heat and mix in remaining ingredients. Press into bottom of a pan and set aside to cool. Cut and serve.

STYLE POINTS: While still warm, form the mixture into the shape of moose scat and, later, convince your companions that's what you are really eating. Be careful if you are traveling with children or you may find them sampling all kinds of wilderness excrement.

CREAMY RICE PUDDING
(SERVES 3-4)

1 cup instant rice

$1\frac{1}{2}$ cups water

2 Tbs. egg powder

$\frac{1}{3}$ cup dry milk

$\frac{1}{4}$ cup brown sugar

$\frac{1}{4}$ cup raisins

$\frac{1}{2}$ tsp. cinnamon or nutmeg

$\frac{1}{2}$ tsp. vanilla (optional)

HELPFUL HINTS: Combine all ingredients in a pan. Bring to a boil and simmer until rice and fruit are tender. Stir frequently as this one likes to scorch. Add more water (preferably hot) if needed.

STYLE POINTS: Serve for breakfast. Or add $\frac{1}{4}$ cup or more hot chocolate for a chocolate dessert.

BAKING REQUIRED DESSERTS

GRAHAM CRACKER SURPRISE
(SERVES 4-6)

1/2 cup margarine

1/2 cup brown sugar

1/2 cup walnuts or pecans

8 graham crackers or their crumbs

HELPFUL HINTS: Mix margarine and sugar in a pan, and bring to a boil stirring constantly. Place the graham crackers in the bottom of your fry-bake pan. Add the nuts to the boiling ooze and pour the mixture over graham crackers. Stove-top bake for about 10 minutes. Let the mixture cool and serve.

COFFEE BARS
(SERVES 4-6)

1/2 cup brown sugar

1 1/2 cups Essential Batter Mix (See Backcountry Baking)

1/4 cup oil

2 Tbs. egg powder

3/4-1 cup strong warm coffee

1 tsp. vanilla (optional)

1 cup chocolate and nut bits

HELPFUL HINTS: Mix all ingredients and pour into an oiled fry-bake pan. Stove-top bake for about 30 minutes.

QUICK AND EASY CAKES

Carry a commercial cake and frosting mix. Most 10 inch fry-bake pans will accommodate only half a normal-sized cake mix (1 1/2-2 cups). Remember adjust for the altitude by adding flour and water. (See Backcountry Baking)

ESSENTIAL CAKE MIX
(MAKES ONE 10" ROUND CAKE)

2 cups flour

$3/4$ cup sugar

$2^1/2$ tsp. baking powder

$1/4$ cup egg powder (optional)

$1/4$ cup milk powder

$1/3$ cup margarine

$1/4$ tsp. salt (optional)

1 tsp. vanilla (optional)

About $1^1/4$-$1^1/2$ cups water

HELPFUL HINTS: Mix all dry ingredients and stir in the wet until batter is smooth. Pour into a well-oiled and floured fry-bake pan. Stove-top bake about 20-30 minutes.

POPULAR VARIATIONS ON THE THEME

CHOCOLATE CAKE: Add $1/4$ cup cocoa, an instant chocolate pudding, or $1/2$ cup hot chocolate mix. Add more chocolate for a richer, darker cake.

CHOCOLATE BUTTERMILK CAKE: Make a chocolate cake (see above) and substitute dry buttermilk for dry milk.

SPICE CAKE: Add 1 tsp. cinnamon and $1/2$ tsp. each nutmeg, cloves, and allspice. Include $1/4$ cup hydrated raisins and $1/4$ cup walnuts or pecans.

APPLESAUCE CAKE: Add one package instant applesauce (Backpacker's Pantry) 1 tsp. cinnamon, $1/2$ tsp. cloves and allspice, $1/2$ cup raisins and $1/2$ cup chopped nuts.

COCONUT PUDDING CAKE: Add an instant coconut pudding mix and cover with Coconut Hailstorm.

TRULY GOURMET CAKES

PMS CAKE
(SERVES 4-6)

$1/2$ devil's food cake mix

$1/2$ package instant chocolate pudding mix

$1/2$ cup dry milk

$1/4$ cup egg powder

$1^1/4$ cup water

1 cup chocolate chips (or as many as you can pick out of the trail mix)

HELPFUL HINTS: Mix all ingredients until smooth. Pour into an oiled and floured fry-bake pan. Stove-stop bake for 30-40 minutes.

FRUITY UPSIDE DOWN CAKE
(MAKES ONE 10" ROUND)

1-2 cups dried mixed fruit

1 cup chopped nuts

4-6 Tbs. sugar

3 Tbs. margarine

1 Essential Cake Batter with $1^1/4$ cups water

HELPFUL HINTS: Hydrate fruit with some hot water (1-2 cups), margarine and sugar in the bottom of your fry-bake pan. Add nuts. Follow recipe for Essential Cake Batter. Pour mixture over the top of the fruit. Stove-top bake until done. 20-30 minutes.

STYLE POINTS: Use apricots and pecans with a chocolate cake. Top with caramel icing.

CRAZY MIXED-UP BOSTON CREAM PIE
(MAKES ONE 10" ROUND)

1 Basic Cake Batter with $1^1/4$ cups water

1 instant vanilla pudding mix

$^1\!/_2$ cup dry milk and 2 cups cold water

1 cup chocolate chips

HELPFUL HINTS: Stove-top bake one Essential Cake Batter. Prepare one instant vanilla pudding mix and set aside to chill. When cake is done, sprinkle with chocolate chips, cover and set aside for chips to melt. Cover with pudding and serve.

FROSTINGS, ICINGS, AND A FEW HAILSTORMS

QUICK TOPPINGS

#1: Carry frosting mix. They come in just-add-water varieties.

#2: Chocolate, carob or butterscotch chips: After cake is done scatter chips on the top, cover and set aside until chips melt. Peppermint Patties work great too, but you'll need to spread them after they soften.

#3: Instant pudding topping: Make pudding first. Set it aside to chill while you bake the cake. Spread on top of cooled cake.

#4: Cover cake with one of the syrups or butters (See Breakfasts).

#5: Sprinkle cake with powdered sugar or cinnamon sugar.

COCONUT HAILSTORM

$1^1\!/_2$ cups coconut flakes

$^1\!/_3$ cup brown sugar

$^1\!/_3$ cup soft margarine

2 Tbs. dry milk or buttermilk

$^1\!/_2$ tsp. vanilla

$^1\!/_4$ cup water

HELPFUL HINTS: Combine all ingredients, spread over top of warm cake, cover until melted.

STYLE POINTS: Build a small twiggy fire on top of the oven to brown coconut.

ESSENTIAL FROSTING ONE

1 Tbs. dry milk

2 Tbs. flour

$^{1}/_{4}$ cup margarine

$^{1}/_{4}$ cup sugar

$^{1}/_{4}$ cup water

$^{1}/_{2}$ tsp. vanilla

HELPFUL HINTS: Heat flour, dry milk and water until very thick. Set aside to cool. Add sugar, margarine and vanilla. Whip with wire whisk or spoon until thick. A whisk is really useful with this one.

ESSENTIAL FROSTING TWO

$1^{1}/_{2}$ cups powdered sugar

$^{1}/_{4}$ cup soft margarine

$^{1}/_{2}$ tsp. vanilla

1 Tbs. dry milk

2 Tbs. water

HELPFUL HINTS: Combine dry and then add wet ingredients slowly. It really doesn't take much water, so be careful.

POPULAR VARIATIONS ON THE FROSTING THEME

CHOCOLATE SAUCE: Add 2 Tbs. cocoa or $^{1}/_{4}$ cup hot chocolate mix.

MOCHA SAUCE: Add 2 Tbs. cocoa and substitute coffee for water.

SPICE FROSTING: Add $^{1}/_{2}$ tsp. cinnamon and a sprinkle of nutmeg and cloves.

TRULY GOURMET FROSTINGS

INTERNATIONAL FROSTING: Add ¼ cup of any of the instant International Coffees to Basic Frosting One or Two. Cafe Francais is a particular hit.

Thanks go to Jennifer Gray Rouillard, Cincinnati, Ohio, who had to take three planes to figure this one out.

CARAMEL ICING

1 cup of sugar

5 Tbs. soft margarine

2 Tbs. dry milk

⅓ cup water

1 tsp. vanilla (optional)

HELPFUL HINTS: Combine sugar, milk and water in a pan. Bring to a boil stirring constantly. Cook until a soft ball starts to form. Remove from heat. Add margarine and vanilla. Beat until creamy. If it's too thick, thin by adding water a teaspoon at a time. If it's too thin, add flour.

STYLE POINTS: Thin out the frosting by adding water. Poke holes in the cake and pour the icing over the top.

RICH FUDGE FROSTING

1½ cups sugar

⅓ cup cocoa or 3/4 cup hot chocolate mix

3-4 Tbs. dry milk

2 Tbs. margarine

½ tsp. vanilla (optional)

¾ cup water

HELPFUL HINTS: Combine sugar, milk, water, and cocoa in a pan. Cook over medium heat stirring constantly until mixture comes to a boil. Boil, stirring very occasionally (only to prevent sticking) until mixture thickens and will become syrup when dropped in cold water. (Try a little drop occasionally in your mug.) At this point, remove from heat, add margarine and vanilla and cool until lukewarm. Beat with spoon until fudge thickens and quickly spread it on cake.

STYLE POINTS: Double the recipe. Spread in a pan and serve as fudge after it cools.

PEANUT BUTTER FROSTING

2 Tbs. peanut butter
1½ cups powdered sugar
1 Tbs. dry milk
2-3 Tbs. water

HELPFUL HINTS: Cream all ingredients together and spread on cooled cake.

CRISPS, COBBLERS, AND PIES

CRISPY FRUIT CRUNCH
(SERVES 4-6)

2 cups of fruit (dried, or any type of edible berry is scrumptious)
½ cup raisins
½ cup nut bits
½ cup quick oatmeal
¼ cup flour
¼ cup brown sugar
1-2 cups reconstituted orange drink (use water and sugar as an option)
¼ cup margarine
½ tsp. cinnamon

HELPFUL HINTS: Combine fruit or wild berries (use less fluid if using fresh vs. dried fruit or berries) and orange drink in bottom of fry bake pan. Bring to a boil and set aside covered. Combine remaining ingredients and spread evenly over fruit. Stove-top bake until crisp. About 20 minutes.

WILD CURRANT COTTLESTONE PIE
(SERVES 4-6)

2 cups currants (or any other edible berry)

1 cup flour

1/2 cup sugar

1 1/2 tsp. baking powder

3 Tbs. milk powder

3/4 cup water

2 Tbs. margarine

HELPFUL HINTS: Combine flour, sugar, baking powder, and milk in a pan. Add water and mix until the batter is smooth. Melt margarine in bottom of fry-bake pan. Pour in batter. Pile berries on top. Stove-top bake until done.

Thanks go to Tim Lindholm, Boulder, CO.

APPLE COBBLER
(SERVES 4-6)

2 cups dried apples

2 Tbs. margarine

1/4 cup brown sugar

1/2 tsp. cinnamon

1 1/2 cups of water

1 cup Essential Batter Mix (See Backcountry Baking)

1/2 cup oatmeal or flour (We prefer oatmeal.)

HELPFUL HINTS: Combine apples, sugar, butter, cinnamon and water in a fry- bake pan. Bring to a boil and simmer until fruit is tender. Meanwhile, mix oatmeal and Essential Batter Mix into a stiff batter. Spoon mixture onto tender fruit and stove-top bake until dough is brown.

ESSENTIAL PIE CRUST
(MAKES ONE 9"-10" CRUST)

1⅓ cup of flour

⅓ cup margarine

3-4 Tbs. cold water

1 Tbs. dry milk

HELPFUL HINTS: Combine all ingredients and work into a ball. Press dough into the bottom and sides of a fry-bake pan.

STYLE POINTS: Double recipe for double-crust pie.

RAISIN PIE
(MAKES ONE 10" PIE)

1 Essential Pie Crust

1½ cups of raisins

1½ cups of water

⅓ cup sugar

2 Tbs. flour

1 cup chopped nuts

1 tsp. cinnamon

½ tsp. cloves (optional)

HELPFUL HINTS: Simmer raisins in water until tender. Add sugar and flour and boil for 1 minute. Add nuts and spices. Spoon onto pie shell. Stove-top bake until shell is done. About 20 minutes.

APPLE PIE
(MAKES ONE 10" PIE)

1 Essential Pie Crust

FILLING:

1½ cups of chopped dried apples

½ cup raisins

2 Tbs. flour

½ cup sugar

2 cups water

TOPPING:

½ cup brown sugar

1 tsp. cinnamon

2 Tbs. butter

½ cup chopped nuts

2 Tbs. oatmeal

HELPFUL HINTS: Simmer apples, raisins, and water until tender. Add sugar and flour and boil 1 minute. Pour into pie shell. Mix all topping ingredients together and crumble onto top of apple mixture. Stove-top bake until crust is done. About 20 minutes.

APPENDICES

CUPS/POUND FOR COMMONLY PACKED FOODS

FOOD (1 POUND)	MEASURE
Almonds, shelled	$3\frac{1}{2}$ cups
Apples, dried	4 - 5 cups
Apricots, dried	$3\frac{1}{2}$ cups
Barley, pearled	2 cups
Beans, black, instant	$4\frac{3}{4}$ cups
Biscuit mix	$3\frac{2}{3}$ cups lightly packed
Butter	2 cups
Bulgur, wheat	$2\frac{2}{3}$ cups
Cashews	$3\frac{1}{4}$ cups
Cheese, Parmesan, grated	$5\frac{1}{3}$ cups
Chocolate Chips	$2\frac{1}{2}$ cups
Cocoa Powder	4 cups
Coconut, dried	4 cups
Cornmeal	3 cups
Couscous	$2\frac{2}{3}$ cups
Cream of Wheat	3 cups
Eggs, dried	4 cups
Falafel, instant	$3\frac{1}{4}$ cups
Farina	3 cups
Fruit Drinks	3 cups
Flour	4 cups
Gelatin, flavored	$2\frac{1}{3}$ cups
Grits, dry	3 cups
Honey	$1\frac{1}{2}$ cups
Hot Chocolate, instant	4 cups
Hummus, instant powdered	4 cups
Lentils	$2\frac{1}{4}$ cups

FOOD (1 POUND)	MEASURE
Macaroni	$3\frac{1}{2}$ - 4 cups
Nonfat dry milk	4 cups
Noodles, egg	8 - 9 cups
Oatmeal	5 cups
Peaches, dried	3 cups
Peanut butter	$1\frac{2}{3}$ cups
Peas, dried split	$2\frac{1}{3}$ cups
Peaches, dried	3 cups
Peanuts, shelled	3 cups
Pecans, shelled	3 cups
Potato Flakes	6 cups
Pudding Mix	3 cups
Raisins	3 cups packed
Refries, instant powdered	$3\frac{1}{2}$ cups
Rice	3 cups
Rice, instant	9 cups
Rice, wild	2 cups
Sesame Seeds	4 cups
Sugar	$2\frac{1}{4}$ cups
Sugar, brown	3 cups firm pack
Sugar, powdered	4 cups
Sunflower Seeds	$3\frac{1}{2}$ - 4 cups
Tomatoes, dry flakes	$2\frac{3}{4}$ cups
Vegetables, dried	5 - 6 cups
Walnuts	4 cups
Wheat germ	4 cups
Wheat bran	4 cups

SUBSTITUTIONS

1 tsp	baking powder	equals	1/4 tsp baking soda + 1/2 tsp cream of tartar
1 Tbs	bouillon	equals	1 bouillon cube
1 cup	margarine	equals	7/8 cup vegetable oil
1 tsp	mustard powder	equals	1 tsp mustard, Dijon
1 tsp	onion powder	equals	1/4 cup onion, fresh minced
1 tsp	onion, minced dried	equals	1/4 onion, fresh minced
1/3 cup	pepper, sweet flakes	equals	1 fresh pepper
1 Tbs	cornstarch	equals	2 Tbs flour
2 Tbs	egg, powdered	equals	1 egg + 2Tbs water
1/2 Cup	fruit, dried	equals	one fresh medium size fruit
1 clove	garlic	equals	1/8 tsp garlic powder
1 Tbs	herbs, fresh	equals	1/2 tsp herbs, dried
2/3 cup	honey	equals	1 cup sugar
1 cup	milk	equals	1/4 cup dried whole milk + 1 cup water

MEASUREMENTS

is equivalent to:

Dash	less than 1/8 tsp
3 tsp	1 Tbs
4 Tbs	1/4 cup or 2 fl oz
8 Tbs	1/2 cup or 4 fl oz
16 Tbs	1 cup or 8 fl oz
2 cups	1 pt or 16 fl oz or 1 lb
4 cups	1 qt or 32 fl oz
2 pts	1 qt
4 qts	1 gal
16 oz	1 lb
1 liter	1,000 milliliters
1 liter (.946)	1 qt
1/2 liter (.47)	1 pt
1 gallon of water	8 lbs
1 12 oz travel mug	1 1/2 cups if filled to lip

CALORIES PER POUND OF COMMONLY USED FOODS

BREAKFAST	Calories/lb.
Cream O Wheat	1658
Granola	2211
Grapenuts	1760
Hash browns-dry	1600
Oatmeal	1672
Wheatena	1618

DINNERS	
Bulgur	1621
Couscous	1600
Egg Noodles	1760
Falafel	2200
Lentils	1860
Macaroni	1674
Potatoes-sliced	1624
Potato Flakes	1650
Refried Beans	2200
Rice	1647
Spaghetti	1674
Tortillas	1200

FLOUR	
Bisquick	1920
Corn meal	1610
Muffin Mix	2280
Sweet Bread Mix	2000
White	1650
Wheat	1651

HIGH CALORIE (HIGH FAT) ITEMS	
Cheddar	1840
Cream Cheese	1600
Mozzarella Whole Milk	1280
Parmesan	2080
Swiss	1680
Sour Cream	1600
Margarine	3200
Oil	4000
Bacon Pieces	2836
Ham	1800
Peanut Butter	2682
Pepperoni	2255
Salami	2041
Smoked Salmon	800
Tuna "water packed"	720
Tuna "oil packed"	880
TVP	1500

TRAILFOOD	
Apples	1102
Apricots	1080
Bagels	1800
Candy-hard	1751
Cashews	2604
Chocolate Bars	1650
Crackers	1828
Coconut	2468
Dates	1243
Fruit Bars	3000
Mixed Nuts	2694
M&Ms	2100
Pita Bread	1000
Peanuts	2558
Popcorn	1642
Power Bars	1600
Raisins	1360
Sunflower Seeds	2550
Trail Mix	2000
Walnuts	2950

DRINKS AND SUGAR	
Brown Sugar	1700
Fruit Crystals	1950
Gatorade	1600
Honey	1379
Hot Chocolate	2000
Jello	1683
White Sugar	1700

DESSERT	
Brownie Mix	1828
Cake Mix	2200
Cheese cake mix	3500
Gingerbread Mix	1928
Pudding	1637

MISCELLANEOUS	
Chicken Base	1117
Beef Base	1082
Corn- dried	1600
Instant Soups: 1 cup	100
Eggs, powdered	2697
Milk-dried, nonfat	1625
Peas and Carrots-dried	1200
Peas and Onions-dried	1200
Peppers-dried	1000
Ramen Soup	1067
Soup Mix-Veggie	1600
Tomato Base	1350

SOURCES OF GEAR AND FOOD

JUST ADD WATER: FREEZE-DRIED AND DEHYDRATED FOODS

Adventure Foods, Route 2 Box 276, Whittier, NC 28789. (704) 497-4113.

AlpineAire, P. O. Box 926, Nevada City, CA 95959. (916) 272-1971.

Backpacker's Pantry, 6350 Gunpark Drive, Boulder, CO 80301. (800) 641-0500.

Campcraft, Ltd., P. O. Box 3553, Ventura, CA 93003. (805) 642-7288. (PouchMate)

Chamy Snacks, 117 West Denny Way #216, Seattle, WA 98119. (800) 322-7010.

Harvest Foodworks, Ltd., 66 Victoria Avenue, Smith Falls, Ontario, Canada K7A 2P4. (613) 284-0777.

Mountain House, Oregon Freeze Dry, P. O. Box 1048, Albany, OR 97321. (800) 547-4060.

Richmoor/Natural High, P. O. Box 8092, Van Nuys, CA 91409. (800) 423-3170.

Sorrenti Family Farms, 1630 Main Street, Escalon, CA 95320. (209) 838-1127.

Traveling Light, Inc., 1563 Solano Avenue, Suite 284, Berkeley, CA 94707. (510) 526-8401.

Uncle John's Foods, P. O. Box 489, Fairplay, CO 80440. (719) 836-2710.

HIGH ENERGY DRINKS AND BARS

AlpineAire, P. O. Box 926, Nevada City, CA 95959. (800) 322-6325. (E-Mergen-C)

Avocet, Box 120, Palo Alto, CA 94302. (800) 227-8346. (Clif Bar)

Champion Nutrition, 2615 Stanwell Drive, Concord, CA 94520. (800) 225-4831. (Cytomax, Cytobar)

Chinook Medical Gear, Inc., 2805 Wilderness Place, Suite 700, Boulder, CO 80301. (800) 766-1365. (Drinks and bars, including Sampler Pack)

FinHalsa Company, 15800 Cedarfort Drive, Santa Clarita, CA 91351. (805) 252-0157. (FinHalsa bar)

Nutritional N-ER-G Products, Inc., 867 South 19th Street, Richmond, CA 94804. (800) 659-7654. (Edgebar)

PowerFood, Inc., 1442A Walnut Street, Berkeley, CA 94709. (800) 444-5154. (PowerBar)

PurePower Sports Nutrition, 10 Mountain Springs Parkway, Springville, UT 84663. (801) 489-3635. (PurePower Bar)

Quaker Oats Company, 321 North Clark Street, Chicago, IL 60610. (312) 222-7560. (Gatorade)

Ross Laboratories, 625 Cleveland Avenue, Columbus, OH 43215. (800) 7-ENERGY. (Exceed)

Weider Food Companies, 1911 South 3850 West, Salt Lake City, UT 84126. (801) 972-0300. (Tiger Sport Bar)

Universal Marketing Corporation, P. O. Box 192, Columbus, MS 39701. (800) 654-1920. (Sqwincher)

STOVES AND FUEL

A&H Enterprises, Box 101, La Mirada, CA 90637-0101. (714) 739-1788. (Camping Gaz, Optimus, Primus: sales and service)

Bibler, 5441 Western Avenue, Boulder, CO 80301. (303) 449-7351. (Hanging Stove)

Coleman Company, P. O. Box 2931, Wichita, KS 67201. (316) 261-3211. (Stoves and fuel: Call or write for the nearest dealer)

Indiana Camp Supply, 125 East 37th Street, Loveland, CO 80539. (800) 759-4453. (Lots of stoves)

Mountain Safety Research (MSR), P. O. Box 24547, Seattle, WA 98124. (206) 624-7048. (XGK, WhisperLite, RapidFire)

Outbound Products, Box 56148, Hayward, CA 94545. (800) 866-9880. (Sigg)

Taymar, Inc., 2755 South 160th Street, New Berlin, WI 53151. (800) 776-7189. (EPIgas)

GEAR FOR THE OUTDOOR KITCHEN

Atwater Carey, Ltd., 218 Gold Run Road, Boulder, CO 80302. (800) 359-1646. (Campside Kitchen and Campside Jr.)

Banks Fry-Bake Company, P. O. Box 183, Claverack, NY 12513. (518) 851-7115. (Banks Fry-Bake Pan)

Coleman Company, P. O. Box 2931, Wichita, KS 67201. (316) 261-3211. (Cookware: call or write for nearest dealer)

Outdoor Research, 1000 First Avenue South, Seattle, WA 98134. (206) 467-8197. (Outdoor Kitchens, Compact and Deluxe)

Stansport, 2801 East 12th Street, Los Angeles, CA 90023. (213) 269-0510. (Cookware)

Strike 2 Industries, Inc., East 508 Augusta Avenue, Spokane, WA 99207. (509) 484-3701. (BakePacker)

Traveling Light, Inc., 1563 Solano Avenue, #284, Berkeley, CA 94707. (800) 594-9154. (Outback Ovens)

WATER FILTERS

General Ecology, 151 Sheree Blvd., Exton, PA 19341. (800) 441-8166. (First Need)

Katadyn USA, Inc., 3020 North Scottsdale Road, Scottsdale, AZ 85251. (800) 950-0808. (Pocket and Mini)

Mountain Safety Research (MSR), Box 24547, Seattle, WA 98124. (800) 877-9677. (WaterWorks)

Recovery Engineering, 2229 Edgewood Avenue South, Minneapolis, MN 55426. (800) 845-7873. (PUR Explorer and Scout)

SweetWater, Inc., 4725 Nautilus Court South, Boulder, CO 80301. (303) 530-2715. (Guardian)

Timberline Filters, Box 3435, Boulder, CO 80307. (303) 494-5996. (Timberline)

ONE-STOP SHOPPING:
EVERYTHING YOU COULD POSSIBLY NEED AND MORE

Campmor, 810 Route 17 North, Paramus, NJ 07653-0999. (201) 445-5000.

Eastern Mountain Sports (EMS), One Vose Farm Road, Peterborough, NH 03458. (603) 924-6154.

Indiana Camp Supply, Inc., 125 East 37th Street, Loveland, CO 80539. (800) 759-4453.

L.L. Bean, 5381 Main Street, Freeport, ME 04033. (800) 543-9089.

Recreational Equipment, Inc. (REI), P. O. Box 88125, Seattle, WA 98138. (800) 426-4840.

INDEX